Joyce Appleby on *Thomas Jefferson*
Louis Auchincloss on *Theodore Roosevelt*
Jean H. Baker on *James Buchanan*
H. W. Brands on *Woodrow Wilson*
Alan Brinkley on *John F. Kennedy*
Douglas Brinkley on *Gerald R. Ford*
Josiah Bunting III on *Ulysses S. Grant*
James MacGregor Burns and Susan Dunn on *George Washington*
Charles W. Calhoun on *Benjamin Harrison*
Gail Collins on *William Henry Harrison*
Robert Dallek on *Harry S. Truman*
John W. Dean on *Warren G. Harding*
John Patrick Diggins on *John Adams*
Elizabeth Drew on *Richard M. Nixon*
John S. D. Eisenhower on *Zachary Taylor*
Paul Finkelman on *Millard Fillmore*
Annette Gordon-Reed on *Andrew Johnson*
Henry F. Graff on *Grover Cleveland*
David Greenberg on *Calvin Coolidge*
Gary Hart on *James Monroe*
Michael F. Holt on *Franklin Pierce*
Roy Jenkins on *Franklin Delano Roosevelt*
Zachary Karabell on *Chester Alan Arthur*
Lewis H. Lapham on *William Howard Taft*
William E. Leuchtenburg on *Herbert Hoover*
Gary May on *John Tyler*
George McGovern on *Abraham Lincoln*
Timothy Naftali on *George H. W. Bush*
Charles Peters on *Lyndon B. Johnson*
Kevin Phillips on *William McKinley*
Robert V. Remini on *John Quincy Adams*
Ira Rutkow on *James A. Garfield*
John Seigenthaler on *James K. Polk*
Hans L. Trefousse on *Rutherford B. Hayes*
Tom Wicker on *Dwight D. Eisenhower*
Ted Widmer on *Martin Van Buren*
Sean Wilentz on *Andrew Jackson*
Garry Wills on *James Madison*
Julian E. Zelizer on *Jimmy Carter*

Jimmy Carter

Julian E. Zelizer

Jimmy Carter

THE AMERICAN PRESIDENTS

ARTHUR M. SCHLESINGER, JR., AND SEAN WILENTZ

GENERAL EDITORS

Times Books

HENRY HOLT AND COMPANY, NEW YORK

Times Books
Henry Holt and Company, LLC
Publishers since 1866
175 Fifth Avenue
New York, New York 10010
www.henryholt.com

Library of Congress Cataloging-in-Publication Data
Zelizer, Julian E.
  Jimmy Carter : the 39th president, 1977–81 / Julian E. Zelizer.—1st ed.
    p. cm.—(The American presidents series)
  Includes bibliographical references and index.
  ISBN 978-0-8050-8957-8
  1. Carter, Jimmy, 1924– 2. Presidents—United States—Biography.
3. United States—Politics and government—1977–1981. 4. Southern
States—Politics and government—1951– I. Title.
  E873.Z45 2010
  973.926092—dc22
  [B]   2010016818

Henry Holt books are available for special promotions and
premiums. For details contact: Director, Special Markets.

First Edition 2010

Printed in the United States of America
1 3 5 7 9 10 8 6 4 2

In memory of my grandparents
Rabbi Nathan and Florence Zelizer
and in honor of all the communities that my grandfather built

Contents

Editor's Note

THE AMERICAN PRESIDENCY

The president is the central player in the American political order. That would seem to contradict the intentions of the Founding Fathers. Remembering the horrid example of the British monarchy, they invented a separation of powers in order, as Justice Brandeis later put it, "to preclude the exercise of arbitrary power." Accordingly, they divided the government into three allegedly equal and coordinate branches—the executive, the legislative, and the judiciary.

But a system based on the tripartite separation of powers has an inherent tendency toward inertia and stalemate. One of the three branches must take the initiative if the system is to move. The executive branch alone is structurally capable of taking that initiative. The Founders must have sensed this when they accepted Alexander Hamilton's proposition in the Seventieth Federalist that "energy in the executive is a leading character in the definition of good government." They thus envisaged a strong president—but within an equally strong system of constitutional accountability. (The term *imperial presidency* arose in the 1970s to describe the situation when the balance between power and accountability is upset in favor of the executive.)

The American system of self-government thus comes to focus in the presidency—"the vital place of action in the system," as Woodrow Wilson put it. Henry Adams, himself the great-grandson and grandson of presidents as well as the most brilliant of American historians, said that the American president "resembles the commander of a ship at sea. He must have a helm to grasp, a course to steer, a port to seek." The men in the White House (thus far only men, alas) in steering their chosen courses have shaped our destiny as a nation.

Biography offers an easy education in American history, rendering the past more human, more vivid, more intimate, more accessible, more connected to ourselves. Biography reminds us that presidents are not supermen. They are human beings too, worrying about decisions, attending to wives and children, juggling balls in the air, and putting on their pants one leg at a time. Indeed, as Emerson contended, "There is properly no history; only biography."

Presidents serve us as inspirations, and they also serve us as warnings. They provide bad examples as well as good. The nation, the Supreme Court has said, has "no right to expect that it will always have wise and humane rulers, sincerely attached to the principles of the Constitution. Wicked men, ambitious of power, with hatred of liberty and contempt of law, may fill the place once occupied by Washington and Lincoln."

The men in the White House express the ideals and the values, the frailties and the flaws, of the voters who send them there. It is altogether natural that we should want to know more about the virtues and the vices of the fellows we have elected to govern us. As we know more about them, we will know more about ourselves. The French political philosopher Joseph de Maistre said, "Every nation has the government it deserves."

At the start of the twenty-first century, forty-two men have made it to the Oval Office. (George W. Bush is counted our forty-third president, because Grover Cleveland, who served nonconsecutive terms, is counted twice.) Of the parade of presidents, a dozen or so lead the polls periodically conducted by historians and political scientists. What makes a great president?

Great presidents possess, or are possessed by, a vision of an ideal America. Their passion, as they grasp the helm, is to set the ship of state on the right course toward the port they seek. Great presidents also have a deep psychic connection with the needs, anxieties, dreams of people. "I do not believe," said Wilson, "that any man can lead who does not act . . . under the impulse of a profound sympathy with those whom he leads—a sympathy which is insight—an insight which is of the heart rather than of the intellect."

"All of our great presidents," said Franklin D. Roosevelt, "were leaders of thought at a time when certain ideas in the life of the nation had to be clarified." So Washington incarnated the idea of federal union, Jefferson and Jackson the idea of democracy, Lincoln union and freedom, Cleveland rugged honesty. Theodore Roosevelt and Wilson, said FDR, were both "moral leaders, each in his own way and his own time, who used the presidency as a pulpit."

To succeed, presidents not only must have a port to seek but they must convince Congress and the electorate that it is a port worth seeking. Politics in a democracy is ultimately an educational process, an adventure in persuasion and consent. Every president stands in Theodore Roosevelt's bully pulpit.

The greatest presidents in the scholars' rankings, Washington, Lincoln, and Franklin Roosevelt, were leaders who confronted and overcame the republic's greatest crises. Crisis widens presidential opportunities for bold and imaginative action. But it does not guarantee presidential greatness. The crisis of secession did not spur Buchanan or the crisis of depression spur Hoover to creative leadership. Their inadequacies in the face of crisis allowed Lincoln and the second Roosevelt to show the difference individuals make to history. Still, even in the absence of first-order crisis, forceful and persuasive presidents—Jefferson, Jackson, James K. Polk, Theodore Roosevelt, Harry Truman, John F. Kennedy, Ronald Reagan, George W. Bush—are able to impose their own priorities on the country.

The diverse drama of the presidency offers a fascinating set of tales. Biographies of American presidents constitute a chronicle of wisdom and folly, nobility and pettiness, courage and cunning, forthrightness and deceit, quarrel and consensus. The turmoil perennially swirling around the White House illuminates the heart of the American democracy.

It is the aim of the American Presidents series to present the grand panorama of our chief executives in volumes compact enough for the busy reader, lucid enough for the student, authoritative enough for the scholar. Each volume offers a distillation of character and career. I hope that these lives will give readers some understanding of the pitfalls and potentialities of the presidency and also of the responsibilities of citizenship. Truman's famous sign—"The buck stops here"—tells only half the story. Citizens cannot escape the ultimate responsibility. It is in the voting booth, not on the presidential desk, that the buck finally stops.

—Arthur M. Schlesinger, Jr.

Jimmy Carter

1

A Maverick Politician

The ceremonial drive from Capitol Hill to the White House that follows a president's swearing-in is, by tradition, a stately procession. Crowds line the approximately mile-and-a-half stretch as the presidential motorcade, accompanied by military bands and mounted units, wends its way down Pennsylvania Avenue to the new leader's new home. On a crystal clear wintry day in January 1977, Jimmy Carter shocked the crowds—and the nation—when he ordered his Secret Service agents to stop the limousine so that he, his wife, Rosalynn, and their nine-year-old daughter, Amy, could join the parade on foot. Stepping out onto the street, Carter thought about "the angry demonstrators who had habitually confronted recent Presidents and Vice Presidents, furious over the Vietnam war and later the revelations of Watergate."[1] Carter, the people's president, was determined not to be seen as standing apart; he was, in fact, more comfortable walking among the citizenry than he was in the formal trappings of presidential power.

Standing in the frigid weather that had gripped the capital that week, the crowd was visibly elated as they watched Carter and his wife stroll the entire sixteen-block walk from the Capitol to the executive mansion. Amy skipped and danced alongside her parents. One man standing at the barricades sporting a long beard that made him look as if he came right out of the 1960s counterculture jubilantly yelled "Jimmy! Jimmy!" The president looked at the man, grinned, and waved his arm. "All right," the man screamed.[2]

Walking among his constituents, Carter appeared to be just the kind of leader a disillusioned nation was looking for. His message was simple: his presidency would be different.

Carter was in fact a genuine outsider who had arrived in Washington after having shaken up Georgia politics as governor. Part of a younger generation of southern politicians, Carter lacked strong ties to major interest groups in the Democratic Party and possessed a stubborn determination that moved him to take politically unpopular positions. His independence and lack of encumbrances were welcome relief just years after the Watergate scandal had weakened public confidence in the political system.

During his first two years in office, Carter did not disappoint. He took the issue of ethics and honesty seriously, supporting procedural and regulatory changes to clean up government. Carter's average approval rating was 69 percent in the first quarter of his presidency (higher than Presidents Barack Obama or Ronald Reagan during this same time period). "Carter has changed the tone for the better," said one Democrat in an interview with *Time* magazine about the first Hundred Days; "he is making the presidency relate to the people again."[3]

The president's popularity was supported by significant early legislative successes. Carter persuaded the Senate to ratify the controversial Panama Canal treaties in 1978, which gave control of the canal back to the Panamanians and signaled a new direction in U.S. policy toward the region. The Senate ratified the treaties by just one-vote margins, but it was a victory nonetheless. His administration also designed an ambitious energy plan, which though severely watered down by the Senate before passage in 1978 is to date one of the most aggressive efforts to come out of the nation's capital to deal with America's dependence on foreign oil and energy consumption. Working with allies in Congress, the administration elevated human rights as a defining issue in foreign policy, aiming to restore moral clarity after Vietnam had shaken Cold War certainties about involvement abroad.

Two years after his inauguration, however, the euphoria about Carter had vanished. This maverick presidency had gone badly. Nothing captured Carter's political problems more than a bizarre story that broke in the summer of 1979 about the president and a Georgia swamp rabbit. Carter had privately recounted this story to a group of staffers who were sitting on the Truman Balcony on a warm spring day in 1979. Carter explained that as he was fishing in a canoe on April 20, a hissing swamp rabbit tried to make his way onto the boat. A photographer had captured the moment. Several months later, Press Secretary Jody Powell informally repeated the story to an Associated Press reporter, Brooks Jackson, over a cup of tea. The next day, Jackson wrote a small piece about the incident and sent it out on the wire, not thinking of the story as more than a humorous piece.[4] The story broke on the front page of the *Washington Post* on August 30. "Bunny Goes Bugs: Rabbit Attacks President," the title read, mocking the unpopular president. What started as an innocent story turned into yet another political headache for Carter.

It was more than two and a half years into his presidency and Carter was in such bad shape that the story actually mattered. Republican senator Robert Dole, who planned to run for president in 1980, joked that Carter should apologize for "bashing a bunny in the head with a paddle. I'm sure the rabbit intended the president no harm. In fact, the poor thing was simply doing something a little unusual these days—trying to get aboard the president's boat. Everyone else seems to be jumping ship." The administration prevented the picture from being made public. "We're afraid if we release the photo," Powell told reporters, "the rabbit controversy over the next two weeks will receive more ink than the SALT treaty."[5]

This was just the tip of the iceberg. For the remainder of 1979 and 1980, the economy was in shambles, oil prices skyrocketed,

Americans were held hostage in Iran, and the Soviets invaded Afghanistan. As the Democratic primaries reached a conclusion and the general campaign of 1980 was about to start in September, the pollster Patrick Caddell warned the president that the race against Republican Ronald Reagan and Independent John Anderson would be difficult.

Caddell's predictions turned out to be correct. Although Carter put up a strong fight in the final month of the campaign, Reagan won, and Republicans regained control of the Senate for the first time since 1954.

· · ·

Most historical accounts of the 1970s have assumed that Carter was inevitably doomed to failure. They argue that Carter was incompetent, weak, and unable to lead. The conventional portrait depicts Carter as a tone-deaf moralist who never displayed many political skills, a man who was fortunate to find himself in the right place at the right time after Watergate and whose weaknesses as a leader became painfully evident as soon as he was given the responsibilities of governing.

But these interpretations ignore some powerful factors that could very well have made Carter a success. His was in fact a presidency with considerable potential. Jimmy Carter was an exceptionally smart man. He could also be very engaging; few failed to be dazzled by his memorably wide smile. And, at least early on, he sometimes demonstrated a real sense of what many Americans wanted, whether that was the desire for an antiestablishment politics or the need for a new moral framework, such as human rights, for debating foreign policy. He was a shrewd political operator who had developed a keen feel for electoral politics, both in Georgia and then nationally, as he successfully defeated powerful incumbents. On many issues, such as race relations and welfare reform, he had the ability to see the potential compromise at a time most liberals and conservatives were moving farther and farther apart. Whereas Senator George McGovern failed in his effort to run a maverick campaign in 1972, losing in a devastating landslide to Richard Nixon, Carter pulled it off.

Carter was also politically appealing as the face of the "New South," the increasingly urban, cosmopolitan, and racially tolerant voices of the region. He was a member of a group of progressive moderate governors, such as John West of South Carolina and Reubin Askew in Florida,[6] who represented the potential for Democrats to regain their hold on the South after the passage of the Civil Rights Act of 1964, legislation that convinced President Lyndon Johnson that he had handed the region to the Republican Party.

Carter was unafraid to innovate, willing to take risks by experimenting with new policy ideas and challenging the orthodoxies of both political parties. From the moment that the oil-producing countries in the Middle East imposed an embargo of oil on the United States, Carter had been quick to understand the arguments about conservation and promoted those goals within his home state of Georgia. While governor, Carter worked with the Trilateral Commission, a group of prestigious experts who wrestled with fundamental changes needed in foreign policy at the confusing stage of the Cold War that came after Vietnam.

Carter was a politician willing to evolve and to question his assumptions. (Critics would later label this a lack of core principles.) Unlike politicians who remained fixed on one set of arguments regardless of circumstances, a problem that helped bring down Lyndon Johnson with the quagmire in Vietnam, Carter applied his background in engineering as a problem solver who adjusted and recalibrated as the political and economic realities changed.

Because he came from the New South, Carter had more political space to pursue these ideas. He was not as tied as other members of his party to the powerful liberal interest groups, including organized labor, who shaped decision making. Carter's political independence and intellectual curiosity seemed to mesh well with an electoral strategy designed to appeal to religious Americans, independents, and even moderate Republicans who had become disillusioned with the political process.

Just as important, the situation was quite good for Democrats, who controlled the White House and Congress for the first time since 1968. Democrats had expanded their numbers in the Senate, reaching the sixty-one majority, enough to end a filibuster.

Yet in the end Jimmy Carter's presidency fell apart. How did someone who had such promise upon entering the White House experience such a terrible outcome? Bedeviled from the beginning of his term by an extraordinarily difficult set of circumstances that would have challenged any president, Carter faced a unique set of personal and political obstacles as well. He struggled with a series of debilitating problems as he made the transition from the politics of campaigning to the politics of governance. And being an outsider in Washington, as it turned out, would be both a blessing and a curse.

2

New Southern Politics

Don't pay any attention to that smile!

—Ben Fortson, 1972

Jimmy Carter was born on October 1, 1924, in Plains, Georgia. Jimmy's father, James Earl Carter, came from a family of successful southern farmers, business entrepreneurs, and landowners, most of whom had embraced the Baptist faith. His mother, Bessie Lillian Gordy, who trained as a registered nurse, was the independent-minded daughter of a local postmaster with progressive views on racial relations.

Four years after Jimmy was born, the Carters moved to Archery, a town located approximately two miles from Plains. Archery made Plains, a town of about six hundred people, look cosmopolitan. It was a sparsely populated rural area consisting primarily of farmland as well as a handful of homes owned by railroad foremen who worked in the area. The local residents tended to walk or travel in mule-drawn wagons.[1] The Carters settled into their newly purchased small wooden clapboard house and 350-acre farm. They grew several crops, including peanuts, which had become the region's major farming industry in the 1920s. Earl and Lillian also owned a warehouse and a grocery store.

James Earl Carter Jr., "Jimmy," was a studious child who avoided trouble. He helped his parents on the farm and in the warehouse, tackling everything from chopping wood to picking cotton. One of his favorite things to do outdoors was to sit with his father in the evenings, listening to boxing matches, baseball games, and political conventions on a battery-operated radio; there was no electricity in their home before the late 1930s.

Earl demanded a great deal from Jimmy and Jimmy's two siblings, Gloria and Ruth. Earl maintained a strict home and sometimes resorted to physical discipline. Some observers blamed his father's tough demeanor for instilling two traits in Jimmy: his propensity to exaggerate accomplishments, which they said came from a desire to please his father, and his ability to smile in almost any situation, which he used to mask anger toward his dad.[2]

The Carters, whose farm in Archery was prospering, belonged to the Plains Baptist Church, a congregation of approximately three hundred members. Earl took his kids to Sunday school and taught classes there. While both parents were religious, they were not teetotalers. Earl liked to drink, party, and dance and Lillian loved to play poker.

African Americans constituted the majority of the population in Archery, and most of the Carters' neighbors were African American. Only one other white family permanently resided in town. White children attended the all-white Plains High School (which started at first grade), while African American children received their education at homes and in churches. But outside of school there was close interaction between the races. Two of Carter's childhood friends, A. D. and Edmund, were African Americans. They played together almost every day and remained close through high school when local norms created pressure for white and black children to sever those bonds.[3]

There were also influential African American adults in Carter's life. After Lillian returned to nursing full time when Jimmy was about five, the children were cared for by an African American woman named Annie Mae Hollis, and Jimmy learned how to farm from one of his father's best workers, Jack Clark. Though Earl would not let him enter through the front door, Bishop William Decker Johnson of the African Methodist Episcopal Church commanded enormous respect throughout Plains and was always welcomed by the Carter family when he came through town.

The Great Depression, which began around the same time Jimmy entered grade school, devastated Plains. While a student, Carter witnessed firsthand how much damage the economic collapse inflicted on the community. The Bank of Plains closed, as did most of the other businesses, and the population fell from six hundred to three hundred. The Carters, however, had more luck than most. Earl was forced to shut his grocery store, but because he lacked debt and had accumulated a sufficient amount of cash, he was able to take advantage of the depressed prices to purchase more land as well as a local insurance and mortgage company.

In his memoirs, Carter recalled the migrant workers who came to their house during the Depression. Lillian frequently invited those passing by to come in and eat if they were willing to do a little work. When one group specifically sought out the Carters for food, Lillian asked how they knew to stop there, since many neighbors were not so welcoming. They said, "Ma'am, we have a set of symbols that we use, to show the attitude of each family along the road. The post on your mailbox is marked to say that you don't turn people away or mistreat us."[4]

Like almost all southerners in this era, Earl was an ardent Democrat. Although he became disillusioned with Franklin D. Roosevelt for being too radical, he remained loyal to the party. In 1937, Earl worked for the Rural Electrification Administration. This, combined with serving on the Sumter County School Board, won him enormous clout in the community. The Carters were doing well financially because of their land purchases and because of New Deal policies that offered subsidies for enclosing open pastures.[5] By the late thirties, Earl had approximately two hundred

African Americans working for him on the farms. In 1937, the Carters had their fourth and final child, who was named Billy.

In June 1941, Jimmy became the first person in his father's family to receive a high school degree. Jimmy's dream was to join the navy, and he applied to the Naval Academy in Annapolis, Maryland. As he waited for the academy's decision, he studied engineering at Georgia Southwestern junior college. Carter obtained a spot at the academy in 1942—Earl used his local clout to persuade Congressman Stephen Pace to secure admission for his son—but, before entering, Jimmy spent a year as a Naval ROTC student at the Georgia Institute of Technology, to receive additional technical training.

· · ·

In June 1943, Jimmy took a train to Washington, D.C. From there, he headed to Annapolis to begin his studies. The first few years at the academy were grueling. His physical limitations—he stood at 5 feet 9, weighing about 121 pounds—made training especially difficult. The social life in this new setting was tough as well. Fellow students at the Naval Academy came to see Carter as an introvert as he did not form many close friendships. And Carter had to endure the type of ritualistic hazing that was then considered routine.

One month after his graduation in June 1946, Jimmy married Rosalynn Smith. Born on August 18, 1927, Rosalynn was raised by a Georgia family of modest economic background. Her mother, Frances Allethea Murray, came from a Baptist family who earned their living through farming, and her father, Wilburn Edgar Smith, was a mechanic and school bus driver. Jimmy's father had his reservations about the match due to his great ambitions for Jimmy, but he did not stand in the couple's way.

Rosalynn had known Jimmy since they were children. Lillian had worked with people in Rosalynn's neighborhood and helped Rosalynn's father before he died from leukemia in 1940. In school, Rosalynn became friends with Ruth Carter and developed a crush on her older brother, though she was initially too shy to say anything. "He seemed so glamorous and out of reach."[6]

Rosalynn finally started dating Jimmy in the summer of 1945 when he was home on leave. She attended the Georgia Southwestern junior college. The independent, shy, and insecure seventeen-year-old Rosalynn turned down Jimmy's first proposal because she wanted to go to the Georgia State College for Women after completing her course requirements at Southwestern (it did not give a formal degree, but rather credits at a four-year college). She was also scared that she was not worthy of being his wife. They privately agreed to wait for a year. After the second proposal, they married on July 7, 1946.

That summer, the two moved to Norfolk, Virginia, where Carter had been assigned to the battleship USS *Wyoming*. The Carters had their first child (John William) in July 1947 and then moved to New London, Connecticut, one year later. The navy had accepted Jimmy into its submarine training program. When he was finished with the program, the navy assigned him to work as an electronics officer on the USS *Pomfret*. The Carters went to Pearl Harbor, Hawaii, where the *Pomfret* was based in March 1949. Rosalynn gave birth to James Earl III on April 12, 1950.

The next stop brought the Carters to Groton, Connecticut, where Jimmy was stationed on the USS *K-1*. During the Korean War, Carter was stationed in San Diego, which Rosalynn found to be unpleasant. Carter's shipmates did not remember him talking about politics other than that he supported President Truman in 1948. Carter later explained his reticence stemmed from the fact that the navy had dissuaded officers from taking political positions.[7]

In 1952, Carter applied for a job to work with Admiral Hyman Rickover on a new nuclear submarine program. Rickover personally interviewed Carter for two hours. Rickover, who rarely smiled, was infamous for adjusting the blinds during job interviews so that the sunlight would shine directly in the face of the candidate.[8] When Rickover asked what his rank was in the Naval Academy, Carter said that he was 59th in his 820-person class. Rickover asked: "Did you do your best?" Carter grudgingly admitted, "I didn't always do my best." Carter survived the interview; Rickover offered him the job.

The Carters, who had another boy in 1952, named Donnel Jeffrey, spent the next year in Washington, D.C., while Carter served on temporary duty at the Naval Reactors Branch, U.S. Atomic Energy Commission. In March 1953, the family moved to Schenectady, New York, where Jimmy took classes in nuclear physics at Union College and prepared to become the engineering officer for the USS *Seawolf,* the second nuclear submarine.

All of these years as an engineer helped to shape Carter's approach to tackling issues. He developed a technical and managerial, as well as a nonideological, mind-set to problem solving that would inform him throughout his career.

• • •

Just when the Carters finally seemed to be settled, Carter learned in the summer of 1953 that his father had pancreatic cancer. Earl died on July 22. Carter decided to leave the navy and move back to his home state. Jimmy's younger brother, Billy, was incapable of caring for the farm, and his mother, Lillian, needed his help as she was suffering from depression because of Earl's death. Carter's decision caused great consternation for Rosalynn, who did not want to return to the South. After some of the worst arguments in their marriage, she finally consented.[9]

By the time the couple returned to Georgia, the Carter family was well established in Archery and Plains. The Carters' farming business and stores were a big economic presence. Earl, already a leader in the community, had even been elected to the state legislature in 1952 and grown close to the governor as a result.

Jimmy and Rosalynn's initial transition to Georgia proved to be difficult. The economy was doing poorly as a result of a drought. Many of the local farmers who had purchased goods from Earl still owed him payments, and Jimmy could not collect because the farmers had no money to pay their bills.

Fortunately, the bad times did not last long. The Carters quickly integrated into the community by joining the Plains Baptist Church and other local civic associations. Once the drought finally ended, the economy picked up, and by 1955 the Carters were doing well financially. Jimmy's income rose to twice what it had been when he had left the navy a few years earlier.

The racial temperature in Georgia heated up following the Supreme Court's *Brown v. Board of Education* decision in 1954. Upon hearing the court's ruling to require the desegregation of public schools, Carter told Rosalynn, "I don't know what's going to happen around here." Many Georgians reacted by protesting or with violence. The most tangible sign of this unrest came with the formation of local chapters of the White Citizens' Council, a group that opposed racial integration and intimidated proponents of it.

Yet Carter never forgot what he learned about the injustices of southern racism from his upbringing in Archery, his mother's progressive views, and the camaraderie he developed while working with African Americans in the close quarters of a submarine. Throughout the 1950s and early 1960s, he rejected invitations to join the White Citizens' Council. Carter further entered the racial thicket in 1961 when he was serving as chairman of the Sumter County School Board. Based on a recommendation from the Georgia Department of Education, the board was considering a proposal to consolidate the Sumter County schools into one system that would consist of a single high school rather than the three all-white high schools. The state argued that the consolidation would be financially efficient and educationally sound. Most of the opposition emanated from segregationists who saw this as a first step toward racial integration.

Carter supported the referendum. On the night after the voting took place, the Carters were attending their son's basketball game in Plains. After hearing an announcement at the game that the referendum had been defeated, they drove back to their home dejected. They found a sign glued to their office door: "Coons and Carters go together."[10]

These kinds of experiences did not leave Carter too excited about local politics. The closest he had ever come to elected office, besides this experience and watching his father, had been to meet with legislators on Capitol Hill in the late 1940s and early 1950s to lobby for naval programs. But Warren Fortson, an attorney and friend of Carter, and Charlie Smith, a local radio station owner, approached Carter on his farm in 1961 to ask him to run against Congressman E. L. "Tic" Forrester, an ardent opponent of racial equality. They believed that Carter stood a decent chance of winning because he seemed intelligent, progressive, and was successful.[11] When the men arrived at the farm, they found Carter dressed in a baseball cap and dirty overalls. After politely listening to the offer, Carter responded that he was too busy with the farm to run for office.

Just as important, southern politics seemed closed off to someone like Carter, who was moderate on domestic issues. In Georgia, state legislative districts were carved up in a fashion that privileged rural voters, who tended to be more conservative, particularly on race relations and policies that were relevant to cities. Though from a rural community, Carter's politics were more in tune with urbanites, a losing stance when communities with sparse and widely dispersed populations were disproportionately represented in the district system.

In *Baker v. Carr* (1962), the Supreme Court ruled that state districts would have to be redesigned in such a way as to avoid diminishing the value of one vote in relation to another on the basis of where a person lived. Atlanta mayor William Hartsfield called the decision the "biggest thing to hit Georgia since Sherman."[12] Following the decision, an Atlanta civil rights lawyer filed a suit in Georgia to challenge the state's process. In May, a federal court ruled that the state's rurally biased county unit system was unconstitutional.

"This was the major news item to be read and discussed at our peanut warehouse, at church, at Lions Club meetings, and in the small county newspapers," Carter recalled.[13] On September 12,

1962, Carl Sanders defeated the segregationist Marvin Griffin to become the Democratic nominee for governor of Georgia. Sanders, who at thirty-seven years old became the youngest governor in the nation, promised to send a reapportionment bill that would create a new, more equitable districting map to the legislature. The hope was that more liberal and moderate urbanites in Georgia would finally have equal say in state politics—and a political door opened for men like Carter who would come to represent this new, more tolerant South.

. . .

The election of Governor Sanders inspired Carter to run for the state senate to represent the two-thousand-square-mile Fourteenth District, which was composed of fourteen sparsely populated communities. On the morning of October 1, Carter woke up and put on his formal dress clothes. Rosalynn immediately noticed and asked her husband where he was going. He explained that he was on his way to the local newspaper to announce his candidacy for the state senate. Despite the lack of warning, Rosalynn supported the decision. There were fifteen days left until the election.

Carter's opponent was a well-known local businessman named Homer Moore who had won election under the county unit system but now had to run again due to the court-ordered changes. Moore was a very good campaigner who delivered strong speeches and drew large crowds.

Moore and Carter had to campaign during the busiest time of the peanut season. Rosalynn was instrumental. She handled most of the family's business during the two-week campaign and called potential supporters on the phone lists. Carter obtained the endorsement of the *Americus Times-Recorder*, owned by his friend's father.

Homer Moore's most influential supporter was Joe Hurst, from Quitman County, one of the state's most powerful bosses. Elected to the Georgia House of Representatives in 1949, Hurst distributed money to loyal candidates and made sure that public works

projects were allocated to his constituents. During one of Hurst's
famous poker games at Atlanta's Henry Grady Hotel, a regular
player, Representative Sam Singer, introduced Hurst to Homer
Moore. Hurst, who suspected that Carter was too liberal on race,
threw his weight behind Moore.

Election Day took place on October 16. As voters went to the
ballot box, Jimmy drove around the district to get a sense of turnout. The problems began when he heard from Rosalynn that her
cousin had witnessed corruption in the Georgetown courthouse
(located in Quitman County). Rosalynn reported that Hurst and
his allies were intimidating residents into voting for Moore. When
one elderly couple entered the courthouse, Hurst greeted them by
telling them how to vote. They defiantly scratched Moore's name
off the ballot. As the couple departed, Hurst yelled that he would
show them how to vote the right way and that if he ever caught
them "voting wrong again" they might find their house burned
down. Hurst stuck his hand into the ballot box, pulled out their
ballots, and threw them into the garbage. He then placed six new
ballots into the box—all with Carter's name crossed out. When
Carter walked into the courthouse, he found Hurst and Doc
Hammond, a physically imposing man, standing next to the ballot
box looking over voters. Carter would later discover that 420 ballots were cast, although 333 were issued. Moore won.[14]

After consulting with attorney Warren Fortson, Carter formally requested a recount of the vote in Quitman County. Atlanta
lawyer Charles Kirbo took on Carter's case. Kirbo was a slow- and
low-talking country gentleman from the Deep South who was
known for driving his old pickup truck into the garage of his sleek
office building. This was the first step in a long-term relationship
in which Kirbo served as an informal adviser to Carter. Kirbo
ordered that the ballot box in question be impounded. Skeptical
of their ability to win, Kirbo also told Carter he would have to
convince the press to publicize his case.

Carter, undeterred, found a sympathetic ear with investiga-
tive reporter John Pennington of the *Atlanta Journal-Constitution*.

Pennington, who had previously written about corruption and the KKK, conducted his own investigation and published hard-hitting stories about the vote fraud that first appeared on October 22.[15] Meanwhile, Carter was assembling his own case. He traveled to Georgetown after each workday to collect as many statements as possible. Carter and Fortson were shadowed by Moore's men, who followed up on Carter's meetings to intimidate residents. The two men were able to amass sufficient evidence, however, to persuade the judge to allow for a recount.

The recount proceedings, which involved numerous courts and party committees, were not resolved until the night before the general election when one judge required that all the counties cross off the names of Moore and Carter and have voters write in their choice. (Two counties refused, leaving Carter's name on the ticket.) Carter and Moore spent the entire next day traveling around the district to reintroduce themselves to voters. Carter won the senate seat, including Quitman County. His first political victory a hard-won battle that reflected his tenacity, Carter also walked away with a lifelong interest in election monitoring and, in a harbinger of political changes to come, an unusual success in standing up to the old-style southern party machine.

• • •

During his first year in the Georgia Senate, Carter was a workhorse, waking early every morning and often arriving first to the building. He fulfilled his campaign promise to read every bill that he voted on. Yet, though he thrived on the opportunity to reshape public policy and serve in a leadership position, Carter did not enjoy the horse trading and socializing that also constituted part of legislative life.

These were exciting years for younger Democrats. Carter was part of a cohort of Georgians who were not beholden to entrenched political machines. Governor Sanders worked closely with them on government reform and higher education, and Carter, in turn, supported most of Governor Sanders's initiatives.

Although he was a segregationist, Governor Sanders cooperated with Presidents Kennedy and Johnson to end massive resis-
tance to school integration and assure Washington that Georgia
would abide by federal laws. Carter, even though he worked on
education, stayed out of the fray in the summer of 1963 as the
civil rights movement came to Georgia. When Student Nonviolent Coordinating Committee (SNCC) organizers mobilized in
Americus, a city in Sumter County, for the first time, several of
the civil rights organizers were thrown in jail. On August 8, SNCC
held a rally protesting segregation with local African Americans
at the Friendship Baptist Church in Americus. The rallies resulted
in police violence, and the events were broadcast on national television. Carter had openly supported President John F. Kennedy,
who was hated in Carter's part of the state for his positions on
civil rights, but that summer Carter avoided making statements,
realizing that most of his constituency opposed the SNCC-backed
protests.

Despite his support for Kennedy, Carter remained popular
among his constituents and his loyalty to the governor brought
him support from the state's political machine. He was reelected
to the state senate in 1964 without any opposition. In January
1966, the press rated Carter as one of the state's most effective
legislators. He could be engaging in his interviews, and his promise to shake up the political system resonated with reporters who
believed in the possibility of a New South.

In early 1966, Carter had been planning to run against Howard
"Bo" Callaway, a segregationist Republican who had won a Democratic congressional seat in 1964. But in May 1966, Ernest Vandiver,
the former governor of Georgia and the favorite for that position,
proclaimed he would not run again due to health reasons. Callaway
then announced that he would switch to the governor's race, and
Carter looked to be a lock for Callaway's soon-to-be-vacated congressional seat.

But Vandiver's decision also gave Carter an idea. All the other
Democratic candidates in the gubernatorial race were politically

conservative, including James Gray, Garland Byrd, and Lester Maddox, and there appeared to be room for a moderate. Carter decided to run for the governorship, consciously positioning himself as a centrist and allying himself with Governor Sanders. When he was asked by reporters whether he was liberal, conservative, or moderate, Carter responded, "I am a more complicated person than that."[16]

Carter assembled a team of talented staffers for his gubernatorial run. One of them, Jimmy Bentley, introduced Carter to the affable and well-dressed Gerald Rafshoon, an Atlanta advertising executive who had recently worked for Twentieth Century Fox in New York. Rafshoon was the consummate public relations man, supremely confident in his ability to shape public perceptions about any given product. Bentley invited Rafshoon to present his ideas on an advertising strategy for the race. At the meeting the next day, Rafshoon proposed a three-week campaign. The voiceover on the ads would state that the experts predicted that Carter could not win and then go on to explain just how Carter would be victorious. Carter's most generous contributor, Bobby Troutman, thought the proposed ads too radical for the time. Rafshoon retorted that Troutman did not understand the new style of campaigning. Rafshoon compared his pitch to the 1960 John F. Kennedy campaign. Troutman said that he knew Kennedy, and this ad campaign was not like Kennedy's; then he left the room. Carter asked Rafshoon to continue with the pitch. He said: "There's only one person you have to satisfy and that's me. I like it." Rafshoon produced ads that focused on the themes of promoting integrity and fighting corruption.[17]

Carter counted on his fresh face and lack of recognition being an advantage in his quest to be governor and took several steps to promote his outsider persona. Carter reiterated the theme in his speeches. "If I ever let you down in my actions," Carter told a group of volunteers, "I want you to let me know about it and I'll correct it. I promise never to betray your confidence in me."[18] He decided that he would not hold a "kickoff" barbecue in an attempt to symbolize that this would be a different campaign than Georgians were used to. He also avoided standard campaign events like large rallies. There were practical considerations behind these decisions. Carter was unsure about how much money he would be able to raise and whether he could draw a sufficient number of people.

The campaign, a long shot to begin with, did not go well. Carter came in third place in the primary. The Democratic victor was Lester Maddox, the segregationist owner of an Atlanta restaurant who had famously barricaded the doors of his establishment and wielded an ax handle to ward off African Americans who wanted service. The New South still had a long way to go in Georgia.

· · ·

Back in Plains, Carter spent the next few years working on his farm. The family business had been steadily growing since Carter's return to Georgia. The year Carter left upstate New York he earned approximately $184 dollars. By 1970, the business was bringing in almost $800,000 a year. Carter was not abandoning politics, but he did need time to recover from his wounds. He was devastated by the gubernatorial loss since he had given up a clear opportunity to win a congressional seat.

Shortly after his defeat, Carter underwent a "born-again" experience, which motivated him to devote his life to Christianity. Carter was also inspired by the work of Reinhold Niebuhr, whose writing imparted to him the message that one of the goals of politics was to use government to create justice in a sinful world. His political vision was taking shape again. In 1967, Jimmy and Rosalynn had a daughter; they named her Amy.

Although he had lost his first race, Carter decided to run again for governor in 1970. He had gained tremendous experience, and Georgians were now more familiar with his name. In 1969, Carter assembled a campaign team that included veterans from the previous run as well as some new faces. This time, they would take no chances. Carter studied every Georgia election since 1952 to try to understand the major trends and data from the 159 counties. The professional pollster William Hamilton, from Washington, helped Carter discern what appearances would be most important. Rafshoon produced another sophisticated television campaign that was put into place a year before the election to promote Carter as a fresh voice in politics.[19]

Since Maddox would be stepping down under the rules of the state that prohibited a governor from occupying the office for two consecutive terms, Carter's main opponent was the former governor Carl Sanders, who had strong support as a result of his tenure and was seen as progressive on racial issues. In fact, many political experts concluded that Sanders's record as governor from 1963 to 1967 and formidable political alliances meant he could not be defeated.

Carter's team thought otherwise. Hamilton Jordan, a volunteer from Carter's 1966 campaign and a fellow Georgian, would be leading the charge. Jordan was brash and absolutely fanatical about politics. He came from a political family and was just a schoolboy when he discovered the thrill of the campaign. "If he didn't run himself," his mother said, "he would run his cousin."[20] Jordan first heard Carter speak in 1966, and although he did not like the speech, he liked the man personally and saw him as someone who could represent the New South, more moderate on race relations and interested in bringing business to the region. He later agreed to become the full-time manager of Carter's gubernatorial campaign.

The veterans were joined by some fresh faces. Stuart Eizenstat, the son of a shoe wholesaler, had grown up in Atlanta. A Harvard Law School graduate, Eizenstat worked as a researcher for Lyndon Johnson and for Hubert Humphrey in his 1968 campaign. It took Carter several meetings to convince Eizenstat to join the team. What ultimately attracted Eizenstat was the notion that Carter could "bridge the historical gap between rural Georgia and urban Atlanta."[21] This tall and quiet intellectual, whose upbringing in cosmopolitan Atlanta and Jewish background brought a different cultural sensibility to Carter's inner circle, was a tireless worker who was willing to spend endless hours researching and analyzing almost every aspect of Carter's campaign.

Peter Bourne was an Englishman who arrived in Georgia through Emory University. After completing his training in psychiatry, he was active in the civil rights movement and was later sent to Vietnam. Upon returning, he joined the Vietnam Veterans Against the War and worked for Senator Eugene McCarthy's presidential campaign in 1968. Bourne was impressed with Carter when they met in 1969. He felt that Carter had the ability to concentrate on a person during an encounter and make them feel as if he was really listening to them. Bourne also thought that Carter would be good for African Americans.

Jody Powell, also from Georgia, was another new figure. Powell, who was raised on a peanut and cotton farm like Carter, had a great wit about him and a gregarious personality. A chain smoker and bourbon drinker, he liked to say that his father taught him the most important things in life: "how to drink beer, drive a tractor and shoot a gun . . . [and] never be ashamed of who you are or where you came from."[22] While writing his doctoral thesis about populism and third-party movements at Emory, Powell contacted Carter to ask permission to interview him. His letter focused on how it would be possible to strengthen the Democratic Party by offering a vision that would compete for George Wallace voters. Wallace was the Democratic Alabama governor who had run as an independent for president in 1968 and who had made his name through his defiant opposition to civil rights. Carter invited Powell for a meeting after reading the letter, and, when they met, Carter asked whether he wanted to work on his campaign. Powell accepted.

The campaign built on themes that were now standard parts of Carter's political repertoire. Sanders posed a particular challenge since he was popular and progressive and had also been known for working to change the political system. Nonetheless, Carter's campaign focused on his promise to help average Georgians, to make government more efficient, and to be responsive to citizen concerns. Carter's appeal was not just antigovernment but was also about winning the support of the political center. This was the combination that Carter sought to define, a populist, anti-establishment centrism, which eschewed the left-right divisions that defined mainstream politics in the 1960s. Adviser and confidant Bert Lance later remarked, "Jimmy was a formidable campaigner. He was a moderate to the moderates, a conservative to the conservatives, and a liberal to the liberals."[23]

Friends had always told Carter that his radiant smile and his ability to charm strangers were big assets. Understanding the importance of personality politics, Carter made his biography central to the campaign. Rosalynn and his mother, Lillian, were familiar faces on the campaign trail.

Yet personality and issues were only part of Carter's campaign. This peanut farmer with a famous grin also showed a tough, if not downright ruthless, side as a campaigner. Carter decided to undercut Sanders's advantage as a popular progressive by painting the former governor as part of a corrupt establishment. Carter questioned Sanders's integrity and suggested that he had used his connections to advance his personal financial interests. He reminded voters that Sanders was a wealthy lawyer who mingled in high social circles.[24]

Carter also painted Sanders as a creature of the left. Carter found out that the company that made the Sanders campaign buttons had manufactured them by using old Hubert Humphrey buttons. The slogan "Count Me For Carl" was inscribed on top of a Humphrey slogan. Carter held a press conference in which he peeled off the Sanders top to reveal Humphrey's campaign words underneath. Although Carter didn't say any more, the point was clear to the reporters: Sanders was a Humphrey Democrat, which among Georgia voters symbolized the left wing of the party.[25] Sanders was unhappy with how a former ally had turned on him and with Carter's willingness to use this kind of campaign for a victory. Decrying Carter's "smear tactics," Sanders called his opponent the "'penny-antiest' politician I've ever come across."[26]

Though neither campaign focused on race, the candidates, even though moderate, could not completely escape the southern politics of race. Carter accepted endorsements from local candidates who were known to be tied to segregationist groups, such as Roy Harris, former chair of Georgia's White Citizens' Council.

On September 9, Carter won 48 percent and Sanders received 37 percent of the vote in the primary. In the runoff election, Carter received approximately 60 percent of the vote. Lester Maddox won the position of lieutenant governor. Hamilton Jordan served as executive assistant to the governor's office, Jody Powell as press secretary, and Charles Kirbo as his informal chief of staff. Carter's inaugural address, which helped mute criticism of his aggressive campaign tactics, focused on ending racial discrimination and reducing poverty.

The editors of the *New York Times* noted with excitement that Carter's address included a promise to alleviate racial tensions. In contrast to previous instances, the promise was publicly offered and warmly received. This was not the traditional back room promise that other southern politicians had made to African Americans. According to the *New York Times*, "Rarely is social change marked by such dramatic symbolism as in the events in Georgia, where Mr. Carter succeeds Gov. Lester G. Maddox, who had risen to political power on the wings of segregationist showmanship."[27] In this and other cases, the continual support of the *Times* would be crucial to building his national credibility among Democratic elites.

• • •

Governor Carter's initiatives were difficult to categorize. As he would throughout his career, Carter refused to be pinned down by preconceptions of what a liberal or conservative should do. His administration pushed for tough criminal laws at the same time that he hired a leading progressive criminal specialist named Ellis

MacDougall to reform the prisons. His major objective was to streamline the state government by eliminating unnecessary agencies and centralizing control under the governor. As expected, the plan elicited significant opposition. Carter sold his program by relying on Rafshoon's public relations campaign and by personally courting key interests throughout the state. The legislature passed much of the reorganization plan. In addition, Carter introduced zero-based budgeting, which forced agencies to rewrite their budgets each year to justify annual spending.

Carter appointed Bert Lance, a close friend, to be the head of the Department of Transportation, one of the most notoriously corrupt agencies in the state. Carter had met Lance in 1970 when he traveled to northwestern Georgia to seek support. The two men hit it off though they could not be more different. Lance was physically huge and socially outgoing. Whereas Carter loved detail, Lance liked the big picture. The son of the president of a small religious college, Lance gained his wealth after marrying the daughter of a prominent banker who had offered him a job. Besides this appointment, Carter depended on Lance to give him advice on other political issues.[28]

Carter continued to refine his image as an outsider. He was only forty-six when he was elected as governor, and he positioned himself as part of a new generation of southerners. On "Speak Up Days," Georgians were invited to come to the mansion to tell the administration about their problems.

The governor continued to tiptoe around the race issue. There were some notable accomplishments, however. His most well-known achievement was hanging a portrait of Martin Luther King Jr. in the state capitol in 1974. In the midseventies, King was still a hated figure among many southerners. Carter also increased the number of African Americans appointed to high-ranking positions in government.

One area of weakness involved Carter's relationship to the legislative branch. Hamilton Jordan noted that his boss didn't "understand the personal element in politics."[29] Carter sometimes leaned too hard in favor of his supporters. For instance, when he convened a postelection meeting with Democratic officials, two prominent party officials—both of whom had endorsed his opponent Sanders—did not receive invitations.[30] Carter also angered legislators when he pushed proposals directly to the public without gauging the political winds in the capital.

Carter's unwillingness to be excessively deferential to local politicians also caused problems. In one incident, Carter invited prominent Democrats to the mansion for dinner. When they arrived, they were served food on paper plates and told to grab drinks from the bathtub. The outraged legislators complained that they were being treated to a "South Georgia barbecue" rather than a formal meal.[31]

Yet Carter was not politically naïve. With a keen understanding of the traditional value of the pork barrel at his disposal, Carter used an emergency budget to distribute funds to legislators. And when the Berrien County school burned down, Carter did not hesitate to instruct his staff that he wanted the legislator from the district to personally ask him for assistance.[32]

The national media started to pay attention to this next-generation, independent-minded governor. *Time* featured Carter in an article about the "new" South. The piece focused on the younger southern governors who were pushing their states beyond racial problems and seeking economic modernization.[33]

Carter's biggest policy accomplishment involved the environment. In 1973, Carter greenlighted a $133 million plan by the U.S. Army Corps of Engineers to build a dam on the Flint River. The dam was supposed to promote economic development and better water use. But Carter discovered from environmental organizations that his administration's initial positive assessment of the dam was flawed. Carter, who grew up enjoying the outdoor life, took a canoe trip through the river and flew over the water with a helicopter, ultimately deciding that he could not allow the dam to be built. In October, Carter vetoed the legislation and teamed up with environmental organizations to block a legislative override.[34]

While he was working in the governor's mansion, an important national development took place that had an impact on Carter's future. In response to the chaos that surrounded the 1968 Chicago Democratic Convention when antiwar student protesters clashed with police in a nearby park, Democrats adopted procedural reforms that allowed suburbanites, African Americans, women, and other minorities to gain a greater role in the nomination process. Primaries and caucuses were declared to be the sole mechanism through which presidential candidates were selected, and states were urged to shift to proportional voting rather than a winner-take-all system. The party also recommended that women, minorities, and young people be represented among the state's delegates in proportion to their populations. The changes signaled the end of the all-powerful party establishment. As party leaders lost the ability to control a majority of the delegates or appoint ex officio delegates, the machine would slowly grind to a halt, opening up the political process to a wave of fresh and much more diverse players.[35]

The first beneficiary of the new system was the person who designed it: Senator George McGovern. Carter did not support McGovern during the 1972 primaries. McGovern had rebuffed proposals for Carter to run as the vice presidential candidate and Carter and his team had taken personal offense.[36] But more important was the fact that Carter believed the senator was too far to the left, especially on foreign policy. Carter and many members of his staff grew up in a region where military service was revered, and Carter thought that McGovern's positions on Vietnam were untenable given how many Americans had fought. "I'd sure as hell hate to have to try to peddle that," Rafshoon said of McGovern's criticism of the war.[37] Carter instead lent his support to Washington senator Henry "Scoop" Jackson, who represented liberals that favored hawkish national security policies. Jackson selected Carter to deliver his nomination speech at the 1972 Democratic Convention in Miami Beach.

It was McGovern, however, who won the day—and the Democratic nomination—in Miami. Upon leaving the convention, emboldened by the way the new winds were blowing, one of Carter's staffers asked out loud, "Why can't Jimmy run for president?" Carter's team all agreed that he should. Peter Bourne wrote a memo suggesting that "the old politicians who think that once McGovern is defeated, it will be politics as usual are dead wrong and do not understand the social forces at work in the country. National political power has become increasingly issue oriented. . . . The people who will win the big prizes are going to be increasingly the people who are willing to take risks, particularly in terms of hazarding existing power bases."[38]

Carter's advisers immediately started devising a strategy for their boss. Jordan and Hamilton believed the time was right for a candidate from outside the political establishment, but one who could not be easily tagged as standing for the left wing of the Democratic Party. In one of several memoranda, Jordan noted that "the strongest feeling in this country today is the general distrust of government and politicians at all levels."[39]

By December 1972, Carter had officially decided to run for president. His advisers recommended that he take a number of steps to improve his chances for victory. One was to increase his name recognition nationally. During a television appearance on the show *What's My Line* in 1973, not one of the celebrity panelists could identify the governor—and they were not even wearing the customary blindfolds. The movie critic Gene Shalit finally guessed that Carter was a governor after asking a series of questions narrowing down the options.

Democrats were in good shape in the summer of 1974. After President Nixon's resignation in August, Congress passed the campaign finance reform acts that created a system of public financing for presidential elections, established a Federal Elections Commission, and imposed contribution and spending limits for candidates. President Gerald Ford's pardon of Nixon in September 1974 for any crimes that he might have committed ensured that the issue of corruption would remain central.

The midterm elections in November, following one of the worst political scandals in American history and at a time of over 6 percent unemployment and over 11 percent inflation, offered Democrats evidence that the next presidential election might very well be about reform. The midterms brought to Congress a class of seventy-five freshmen who were ready to shake up Washington. They wanted to change the way campaigns were financed, open up government to public scrutiny, and create rules and regulations that imposed restraints on every elected official who held power. The message was clear: there would be no more Richard Nixons. Taking immediate action to ensure that the reforms would take hold, the "Watergate Babies" quickly deposed four powerful committee chairmen, thus ushering in new leadership and ending "the tyranny of the committee chairmen."[40]

Soon after the midterm campaigns, Senator Walter Mondale of Minnesota announced that he would not run for the presidency. Mondale had been considered the Democratic candidate with the best chance of rebuilding the New Deal coalition. But Mondale's exploratory committee had met with lukewarm success. The other two Democratic giants, Senators Ted Kennedy and Hubert Humphrey, decided not to run, leaving the party without a natural establishment figure for 1976.

Carter met with House Majority Leader Tip O'Neill following the midterm elections. One of the first things that Carter told him was "I'm going to be the next president." He told O'Neill that without Kennedy, Humphrey, or Mondale in the race the Speaker could give his support to a southerner. One of O'Neill's aides said that despite Carter's self-confidence, the majority leader "just did not take him seriously."[41]

· · ·

On December 12, 1974, Carter formally announced that he was going to run for president. When Carter began to prepare his campaign, he still did not have a natural base of support. While environmental activists joined in his campaign, he had only thin alliances with organized labor, civil rights organizations, and even

Democratic officials. The strategy was to thus run the same kind of outsider campaign that had been successful when he ran for the Georgia Senate in 1962 and for the governorship in 1970. In 1975, Carter published an autobiography entitled *Why Not the Best?*, which sold almost 1 million copies and helped build his grassroots support.

The governor had built an entire career around positioning himself as a political outsider. Just as the one-man one-vote Supreme Court decisions upset southern politics and allowed a candidate such as Carter to succeed, Watergate opened up the possibility for a candidate who was not intimately tied to the party establishment. This was the year for a maverick. Jimmy Carter's moment had arrived.

3

The Outsider Wins

I owe the special interests nothing.

—Jimmy Carter, 1976

When the race for the presidency began in the winter of 1975, Carter faced a long list of opponents, and an uphill battle to defeat them. After Richard Nixon's dramatic downfall, Democrats felt optimistic about winning the White House for the first time since 1964. President Gerald Ford had helped move the nation beyond Watergate, but his stumbling performance and inability to revitalize the economy did not bolster the faith of Republicans. Without Walter Mondale or Ted Kennedy running, and with Minnesota senator Hubert Humphrey refusing to declare his candidacy, lesser-known candidates had an unexpected chance.

Still, the odds were on an establishment figure winning, particularly after the insurgent George McGovern's disastrous defeat to Richard Nixon in 1972. Arizona congressman Morris Udall stepped up in November 1974 to take Mondale's place as the liberal candidate who could reunite the fractured Democratic Party. Udall enjoyed a famous political name (his brother had been

President Kennedy's secretary of the interior) and had built his reputation in the House of Representatives by championing popular middle-class causes such as the environment. Udall was not the only candidate who invoked the Kennedy name. Sargent Shriver, well known as Senator Ted Kennedy's brother-in-law and the entrepreneurial leader behind landmark 1960s programs such as the Peace Corps, also threw his hat into the ring.

Indiana senator Birch Bayh positioned himself as the experienced Democrat who was most electable. Good-looking and energetic, Bayh combined intelligence with folksy appeal. Observers felt that Bayh had one of the best chances to pull loyal Democratic voters and organizations into his fold. Bayh's colleague Senator Fred Harris of Oklahoma had also decided to run. Harris's campaign aimed to appeal to George Wallace supporters, who were attracted by populist rhetoric but who had abhorred Wallace's racist positions.

Terry Sanford, the former governor of North Carolina and president of Duke University, likewise wanted to pick off Wallace and Carter supporters by pitching himself to new southerners who were more interested in a booming economy than reliving memories of the Civil War. Senator Frank Church of Idaho was a solid New Deal liberal who gained national attention by leading the opposition to the Vietnam War and by chairing high-profile Senate hearings into wrongdoing by the CIA.

There were also candidates who ran more conservative campaigns. George Wallace, who sat crippled in a wheelchair as a result of an assassination attempt and could barely hear, felt that his celebrity stature combined with a solid victory in Florida would allow him to be a serious contender for Democratic delegates. Washington State senator Henry "Scoop" Jackson sought to appeal to New Deal liberals who believed that their party had become too dovish on foreign policy as a result of Vietnam. Texas senator Lloyd Bentsen represented the dying breed of southern conservative Democrats with close ties to the oil industry.

· · ·

Carter realized that in order to break free from the pack, he would have to attract national media attention early on and to develop a strong grassroots presence in caucus and primary states. No Democrat could depend any longer on simply wheeling and dealing with the party bosses who once controlled the delegates at the convention. The 1972 reforms transformed the nomination process into something that resembled a general election campaign rather than a smoke-filled back room meeting; voters now directly decided through primaries and caucuses which candidate would receive the delegate vote. Under the reforms, moreover, the Democrats adopted proportional voting so that the loser of the majority vote in a state still walked away with a number of delegates that could be important in the long-term count.

Since the primaries and caucuses took place over the course of several months, Carter realized that momentum would be a crucial factor. Victory in one caucus or primary, no matter how small, would help to create the impression of a viable candidate in the next round of voting.

Fund-raising reforms also presented both a challenge and an opportunity for lesser-known candidates without easy access to money. President Ford had grudgingly signed campaign finance reform legislation into law on October 15, 1974. According to the new laws, candidates could qualify for public financing if they raised at least $5,000 from private donors in a minimum of twenty states, with a cap on individual donations at $1,000. While Jackson and others focused on raising as many big donations as possible before the rules went into effect, Carter decided to work within the new system. He attended fund-raising parties throughout the states and employed the direct mail techniques that conservative activists had introduced in the 1960s.[1] His campaign sold T-shirts, peanuts, and other souvenirs for small amounts of money, and his staff organized rock concerts with groups such as the Allman Brothers Band and the Marshall Tucker Band. Carter appeared on stage at the concerts to ask attendees for names and addresses for further solicitations.[2] Despite not having access to the biggest donors, Carter raised enough money to qualify for federal funds, which in turn enabled him to organize a serious campaign.

The campaign's first test was Iowa, which was holding its caucus on January 19. Carter and Jody Powell had started visiting the state almost a year before. In early 1975, Carter and Powell had read an article in the *Des Moines Register* that reported, based on initial interviews with caucus participants, how much Iowans liked Carter. The article gave them an idea. Here was a huge opportunity. Based on the *Des Moines Register* reports, Carter had a real shot at victory.[3] Even better, however, a victory in Iowa could change the dynamics of the contest. If Carter succeeded in this early heartland state, he would make a name for himself, the media would write him up as a serious candidate, and he could go into New Hampshire looking like a winner. Carter decided to make several early trips to the state.[4]

At that time, most Democrats did not devote serious organizational resources to Iowa. They were focused on New Hampshire, the traditional launch of the campaign season. After all, Iowa claimed only 47 out of 3,008 delegates. Tim Kraft, Carter's chief organizer in the state, however, embraced Powell and Jordan's view of the opportunity Iowa offered and initiated a very different approach. A skilled political hand who had been recruited into the campaign to establish the groundwork for an early victory, Kraft had already participated in an impressive list of campaigns around the country. He immediately set up twenty state-wide committees, each charged with finding volunteers for the Iowa caucuses who could inform neighbors about Carter and help transport people on the day of the caucuses.

Nobody ever paid much attention to Iowa's Jefferson-Jackson Day fund-raiser. In election years, the annual fund-raiser kicked off the Iowa caucuses, a somewhat bizarre and complicated political tradition whereby Iowans met in homes and schools to decide which candidates should receive their support at the Democratic Convention. Kraft, however, decided to treat the Jefferson-Jackson

Day fund-raising dinner in December 1975 as seriously as other candidates treated Election Day. He arranged for volunteers to provide transportation, and since the dinner at $50 per couple was expensive, he struck a deal that allowed Carter supporters to sit in the balcony and watch. For $2, they got "everything but the chicken dinner." On the night of the dinner, Rosalynn and some volunteers walked up to the balcony and distributed large campaign pins to hundreds of people who were sitting in the front rows. Their goal was to create a good image for the local television cameras. Kraft said: "Politics is theater. We planned for that."[5]

The strategy worked beautifully. Subsequent polls showed clear support for Carter, and the national media published articles proclaiming that Carter had emerged as a major contender. "Whether he can maintain his early lead here when the contest switches from opinion leaders to rank-and-file voters is unclear," wrote R. W. Apple of the *New York Times*. "What is evident is that Mr. Carter, working from Atlanta rather than Washington, has made dramatic progress."[6] Things were off to a promising start.

The Carter campaign continued the full-court press. Carter personally knocked on doors and left handwritten notes for people who were not at home. Tagging alongside him, Powell collected the names and addresses of Iowans whom Carter did meet so that the governor could send them personal thank-you notes.

Carter promised policies that appealed to broad cross sections of the party, including those who normally opposed each other. He talked about the need to make government less wasteful in order to balance the budget while also endorsing more government assistance to deal with unemployment. Liberals were happy with his proposals to cut defense spending and to reform the CIA at the same time that religious conservatives were excited about his embrace of Christianity.[7] "On social justice, human rights, the environment, I would be quite liberal," Carter liked to say. "On questions dealing with the management of Government, I would be quite conservative." In the end, his most important claim was trust. "If I ever lie to you, if I ever betray you, then I want you to leave me," Carter said.[8]

Retail politics and media appearances were not the only factors at work. Carter campaigned like an outsider but didn't always act like one. He sometimes courted traditional Democratic supporters, such as organized labor. During McGovern's 1972 campaign, labor leaders had been excluded from the nomination process. McGovern and his followers had seen organized labor as part of the establishment against which they were rebelling. This time around, unions decided that they needed to make themselves a force in the Iowa caucuses, which, like most politicians, they had not taken seriously in the past. While much of the labor movement remained leery of Carter, he was able to win the backing of the United Auto Workers once their president, Leonard Woodcock, announced his support for Carter in the Iowa caucuses. He and others in the state were impressed by Carter's performance with small groups and his intellectual firepower. More importantly, Woodcock sensed that Carter's southern identity might offer an advantage over the other candidates.

The other major Democratic candidates did not devote much time to Iowa until the final stretch. Udall sent in campaign professionals, but only after the kickoff fund-raiser, and by then it was too late. Bayh plunged into the state toward the very end when he realized he was likely to lose. The Bayh campaign put together a desperate last-minute effort as they realized that a loss would undermine their candidate's claim to be the most electable.

On January 19, Carter defeated Bayh by a two to one margin. Jackson, Harris, Udall, and Shriver did not come close. The most votes went to "uncommitted," but Carter won more than the other Democrats. "My husband and I wanted a fresh face and a new approach," said one woman from Davenport. "We wanted somebody who could clean up the mess in Washington because he wasn't part of it."[9] The shrewd Carter did not go to Iowa the night of his victory, but rather was in New York. Carter had anticipated the win, and being in New York City allowed him to speak with reporters from the major news networks the following morning, including appearances on the morning news shows of all three major networks.[10] The media ate the story up. Though some reporters, like Elizabeth Drew, ridiculed Carter as inauthentic, many others felt that his unexpected rise to fame played well on the tube, and the networks gave his victory a lot of airtime.[11]

• • •

The next contest was New Hampshire. The Carter campaign employed the "Postcard Plan," whereby volunteers were invited to headquarters in order to fill out postcards to send to friends and neighbors. On the postcards, volunteers recounted having met Carter and explained why they supported him. Using language provided by the campaign, volunteers spoke about him as a friend and neighbor, emphasizing his personal qualities and ethical values as much as his professional attributes. Carter promised New Hampshire residents that "I'll never tell a lie, I'll never avoid a controversial issue." Yet the campaign simultaneously played up his celebrity qualities. In their television commercials, Rafshoon cultivated the similarities that he saw between Carter's physical appearance and that of John F. Kennedy.[12]

To the frustration of his opponents, Carter dominated the press coverage. The New Hampshire primary had turned into a media circus. The three major networks sent over four hundred people and twenty camera crews. Carter's blend of local organizing and media-savvy campaigning worked well. To reach out to as many primary voters as possible, Hamilton Jordan sent a group of ninety-eight volunteers, most of whom knew Carter personally, from the Atlanta headquarters to New Hampshire in January. The "Peanut Brigade," as they were called, swept through the state for one week and created a huge media sensation. The volunteers broke up into small cohorts, each armed with a map of the state that contained home addresses for registered Democrats. They made contact with almost twenty thousand homes and appeared with President Carter at a rally in Manchester; they drew on this tactic from Carter's 1970 gubernatorial campaign, when they had done the same thing at the state level. After they returned to Georgia, the volunteers wrote letters to all the families with whom they had met. *Newsweek* published a story about them on February 2, noting that the Brigade had made the "most dramatic impression in the campaign so far by fielding a force of 98 Georgians to sing his praises door-to-door all over snow blanketed New Hampshire."[13]

More than anything else, Carter used his own story to great effect on the campaign trail. His autobiography—his origins in the small town of Plains, his hard work as a child, his progressive mother and disciplinarian father, his family peanut business and career in the navy—were his greatest assets, and he constantly discussed them before crowds.[14] He never failed to stress his southern roots at a moment in American history when the national culture was becoming enamored with the New South, from southern rock to stock car racing. One Republican noted that "Carter is playing upon two essentially conflicting myths—the 'good ole boy' rural South and the 'black and white together' new South."[15]

With all the media attention came some negative press coverage as well. As reporters started to take Carter more seriously, they also started to raise more questions about his claims. In an article entitled "Jimmy Carter's Pathetic Lies," Steven Brill, writing for *Harper's*, charged that Carter was much more of an opportunist than voters suspected, "a very smart, hard-working, tough politician who's campaigning as an antipolitician."[16] The article accused Carter of running a dirty tricks campaign against McGovern in 1972, and it provided an unflattering interpretation of his 1970 gubernatorial campaign in Georgia.[17] When Carter, who had seen an advance copy, was asked about the article at a press conference on February 1, he called it a "collection of lies, distortions, and half-truths."[18] The *Boston Globe*'s editor, Thomas Winship, allowed Jody Powell to publish a lengthy response in the paper when the *Globe* published excerpts from Brill's article.[19] Powell's response was sufficient, and the benefits of the media still outweighed the costs. New Hampshire Democrats voted for Carter. Udall took second place and Bayh came in third.

In Massachusetts, Senator Jackson organized an unexpectedly strong campaign. "I got the lunch-bucket vote and some of the liberals." Jackson claimed that, unlike his opponents, only he could restore the "Grand Coalition" of ethnic groups, unions, and liberals that had elected Presidents Roosevelt, Truman, Kennedy, and Johnson.

Caddell and Rafshoon nervously sat on an airplane landing at Boston's Logan Airport on the afternoon of the Massachusetts primary. Neither of them was sure what would happen. When Caddell saw the amount of snow that was falling, he lamented, "There went our lead." Based on their polling data, Caddell, Jody Powell, and other staff had concluded that Carter attracted a "soft" vote. This meant that Carter's strength resulted from momentum and expectation rather than deep-rooted loyalty. The "soft vote," said Powell, "is the voters who don't care enough to come vote for you in the rain."[20]

He was right. Carter came in fourth place, losing to Senator Jackson.

The Florida primary on March 9 was a crucial test for Carter. Equally important as regaining momentum after the loss in Massachusetts was Carter's need to defeat George Wallace. Since 1974, Carter, Jordan, and Powell had worried about how Wallace would perform in Florida, a state where the former Alabama governor could attract a sizable block of Democrats. With Jackson emboldened in Massachusetts and Wallace running in more comfortable territory, Carter confronted the first primary where he could not easily position himself as the moderate or conservative alternative to the liberal wing of the party.

Carter's campaign again combined strong organizational mobilization with intense television advertising. Carter won Florida with Wallace falling further behind in the delegate count. Carter did better than his opponents with Democrats of all social categories, income levels, ages, and political ideologies.[21] Other than

Jackson, who finished in third place, there was no longer a viable candidate who could appeal to Democrats worried about the liberal direction of the party. When Wallace lost again in North Carolina on March 23, Carter secured his position as the main "southern Democrat" in the race.

Following his victory in North Carolina, the "antiestablishment" Carter demonstrated that he was attuned to political realities and not some naïve antiestablishment southern populist. In late March, Carter attended a dinner party in the Georgetown section of Washington, D.C., hosted by the columnist Clayton Fritchey. Others in attendance included the publisher of the *Washington Post*, Katharine Graham, CBS commentator Eric Sevareid, former defense secretary Clark Clifford, and a larger group of prominent insiders. Carter worked the tables as he schmoozed with guests about key issues such as the Middle East and deregulation. He made a favorable impression among most of those in attendance.[22]

Carter spoke to the Congressional Black Caucus (CBC). Many of the attending legislators were suspicious of Carter, given his southern origins and media accounts of how he had used racial issues to his advantage. Carter was the last of the Democratic candidates to meet with the CBC. One of the questions that the representatives asked each candidate was "How many blacks do you have on your staff?" All of the candidates had answered "one" with the exception of the most liberal Democrat, who said he was trying to find someone to employ. When the CBC representative asked Carter this question, a staffer interjected to answer, "Twenty-seven." The caucus was impressed.[23]

• • •

In between Florida and North Carolina, Carter had to contend with the machine-dominated politics of Illinois and Mayor Richard J. Daley of Chicago, the boss of the Cook County machine. Most of the Democratic presidential candidates did not run in Illinois because they were scared of Daley. Daley was determined to control enough delegates at the national convention to be able to influence party decisions. In Illinois, Carter won over the mayor by not opposing most of Daley's handpicked delegates in Cook County but instead focusing on the delegates throughout the rest of the state. Carter reached an agreement with the mayor whereby his supporters would vote for Daley to head the Illinois delegation at the convention. The deal worked and Carter won 70 percent of the races outside Cook County, even winning a handful of races in Daley's upstate territory. The victory in Illinois boosted Daley's impression of Carter's skills: "His was a campaign that some respect must be paid to."[24]

Despite the Illinois victory, Carter still had to win in a major northeastern state where all the candidates were running in order to demonstrate that he would be a viable contender.[25] Carter had reason to be worried. He had to eliminate Senator Jackson, who had won the New York primary. And adding to his troubles, Carter made a damaging gaffe in New York when on April 2, during an interview about school busing, he told a reporter, "I see nothing wrong with ethnic purity being maintained. I would not force racial integration of a neighborhood by government action." The statement appeared to support white urban opponents of school busing who had been protesting court-ordered integration in cities such as Boston.

Pennsylvania turned into a major test for Carter. His advisers were concerned that the ethnic purity remark could cost him the state. Andrew Young, a prominent civil rights activist and the first African American from Georgia elected to Congress since Reconstruction, urged him to apologize. Young had given his support to Carter when many African Americans were still suspicious of the governor's background. In Philadelphia, Carter said that he regretted making the statement. But tension with liberals and African Americans remained as many suspected he had made the statement to appeal to conservatives.

The party machine threw its support behind Senator Jackson. But Jackson had taken Pennsylvania for granted. He counted so much on his support from the state Democratic bosses that his own organizational efforts were limited.[26] Also, Jackson's coffers were barren since he had spent too much money in Florida and Massachusetts.

In contrast, Carter ran a strong operation. His efficient management of his money had left him with enough funds to run all the advertisements that he needed.[27] Tim Kraft recruited large numbers of volunteers to knock on doors and make almost three hundred thousand calls.[28] Carter won the primary with 37.2 percent of the vote. With his victory in Pennsylvania, along with Florida, Vermont, Illinois, New Hampshire, and Iowa, Carter had placed himself in a strong position.

• • •

A significant challenge to Carter emerged when Senator Frank Church and California governor Edmund "Jerry" Brown finally entered the race. Church was depending on the fact that his Senate investigation of the CIA gave him substantial name recognition, and, indeed, Church won in Montana and Nebraska.

Brown posed an even greater threat. The governor of California was a western, hipper, and more cosmopolitan version of Carter. Like Carter, Brown (the son of the well-known former governor Edmund "Pat" Brown) embraced the image of a politician who did not seek the formal trappings of power. He drove to work in a state-owned sedan rather than a limousine, lived in an apartment rather than the governor's mansion, and practiced Zen Buddhism. Brown expressed his sympathy toward social and cultural liberalism while simultaneously emphasizing the limits of government intervention. He combined promises to protect public land with assurances that he could balance the budget. Fusing populism, antigovernment rhetoric, and suburban liberalism, Brown told supporters that Americans lived in an "era of limits." Carter responded by making even stronger statements against government, but the strategy backfired in Maryland, where many government workers resided.[29] Brown pulled off a huge upset in the state, soundly defeating Carter by 48.3 percent to 36.9 percent.

Church flexed his muscles in the Oregon primary. On May 25, there were six primaries, but only Oregon was competitive. Church mounted a skillful campaign and defeated Carter. The results offered further evidence that Carter had not wrapped up the nomination. The Georgian couldn't win over voters in the West. Seeking to sway media coverage after the loss, Carter flew back to New York. By speaking with reporters about all six races as the primary results were coming in, he hoped to deflect attention from Oregon.

Jody Powell offered David Nordan, an editor for the *Atlanta Journal*, an exclusive opportunity to sit with the candidate in his New York hotel room.[30] During Nordan's time in the suite, he overheard Powell discussing a statement that Senator Kennedy had made earlier about Carter being "indefinite and imprecise" on purpose. Carter's instant reaction was that he was happy he didn't "have to kiss Teddy Kennedy's ass to win the nomination." The following day Nordan put the quote on the front page, and the Associated Press picked it up.[31]

The race came to a conclusion on June 8 with the New Jersey, Ohio, and California primaries. Carter assumed that he could not win California with Brown in the race. So he focused all of his attention on New Jersey and Ohio. The night before the primary, Carter realized that he would lose in New Jersey to Brown. But in Ohio, an industrial economy with large numbers of rural voters who had moved there from the South, he would likely win.

With the outcomes of the races too close to be determined, Carter turned his attention to the press. Carter sensed there would be a lot at stake in how the media reported on the primaries. A front-runner losing two big Democratic primaries so late in the campaign could be devastating and could easily be interpreted as a sign that the contest should be resolved at the convention. On the morning of the primary, Carter asked Mayor Daley if he would commit to Carter's candidacy if he won Ohio. After their conversation, Daley told reporters that if Carter won in Ohio, he deserved to be the party's candidate. Daley's statement was powerful because it came from a quintessential party official and established a standard favorable to Carter by which to judge the returns.[32]

The evening ended with the expected Carter victory in Ohio. While attending a rally at 2:15 a.m. in the Hyatt Regency of Atlanta, Carter received a call from George Wallace. Wallace was releasing his 171 delegates in support of the Georgia governor, giving Carter the number of delegates that he needed for the nomination. Claiming a victory based on Wallace's endorsement, however, would be dangerous politically because it would link Carter's success to the southern demagogue. Carter put in a call to Senator Jackson, who agreed to instruct his 248 pledged delegates to back Carter as well.

Carter had always been very successful with the media, where image and symbols mattered. Now he faced a new challenge. He was no longer going to be seen by reporters as the maverick. Henceforth, he would be the official candidate. Before appearing with reporters to inform them that he had the delegates needed for the nomination, Carter changed his clothes. Donning his trademark blue jeans and jean jacket, he signaled his new message. He was about to become the establishment figure for Democrats, but he would still be "the underdog fighting the establishment."[33]

• • •

While the Democrats finally settled on their candidates, the Republicans struggled through a fratricidal primary between Gerald Ford and Ronald Reagan that had divided the party between moderates and conservatives.

The final results could not be seen as a mandate. Ford secured the nomination, by the narrow margin of 1,187 to 1,070 votes. Even though Ford had won, he had depended heavily on the incumbent advantage to do so. Further, Reagan had defined the terms of the contest and profoundly influenced the agenda of the GOP by moving it rightward. "Reagan was the dominating presence of the 1976 campaign," concluded William F. Buckley Jr., "even though Ford was the formal victor."[34]

Robert Teeter, Ford's pollster, was dejected following the hard-fought primary. Teeter wrote an internal analysis arguing that Democrats enjoyed a huge advantage with votes and money. While Carter had many negatives, voters also saw virtues, such as his stronger personal appeal, his fight against the corruption of Washington, and his concern about the fate of average Americans. Whereas Ford's supporters liked that he was responsible and had proven that he could fight against the Democratic Congress, his sizable negatives included his lack of a vision, his ties to the Washington establishment, and his inability to gain control of government or the economy.[35]

• • •

In contrast to the Republican candidates, Carter enjoyed relative harmony at the Democratic Convention in New York. The party was pleased to have selected a southerner for the first time since 1964. Many labor and Democratic activists were nervous about Carter since they did not know him personally; nonetheless, the AFL-CIO supported his candidacy.[36]

The best interview Carter had with a potential vice presidential running mate took place with Senator Walter Mondale, who Carter had originally thought would be far too liberal and too much of an insider. Determined to win Carter's support, Mondale studied everything about him and came prepared with a meticulous presentation about how he could help the ticket. Carter was energized by their encounter and chose the Minnesotan. The choice received mixed responses. Liberals such as Tip O'Neill were pleased. Conservatives in the party were not. George Wallace said that he felt "sorta mixed—like a father seeing his daughter come home at 4 o'clock in the morning with a Gideon Bible tucked under her arm."[37]

During his convention acceptance speech, Carter called for

revitalizing America's government without becoming too depen-
dent on its policies. Quoting one of the most popular songwriters
of the time and trying to tap into the same cultural energy from
younger Americans that George McGovern had been able to
attract, Carter said, "I have never had more faith in America than
I do today. We have an America that, in Bob Dylan's phrase, is
busy being born, not busy dying." Carter promised that if elected,
the country could have "an American President who does not
govern with negativism and fear of the future, but with vigor and
vision and aggressive leadership—a President who's not isolated
from the people, but who feels your pain and shares your dreams
and takes his strength and his wisdom and his courage from you."
He would be, in other words, the anti-Nixonian president.

Carter was optimistic about his prospects in November.
Besides Ford's mediocre performance in the White House and the
divisions that had opened up in the GOP primaries, polls showed
that Carter had pulled ahead by thirty-three points.[38] Carter
launched his campaign from Warm Springs, Georgia, where
Franklin Roosevelt had vacationed during his presidency. Carter
promised that he, like Roosevelt and Kennedy, could provide the
leadership that was missing in the White House. "It's time for a
change," he said. Carter personally added a line to the speech: "I
owe the special interests nothing. I owe the people everything."[39]

· · ·

From the start of the campaign for president, Hamilton Jordan
stressed the need to emphasize issues and personality, and he gave
little attention to winning the support of members of Congress.
Carter, Jordan felt, had to distance himself from Washington.[40]

The kind of campaign that Jordan outlined for Carter directly
contrasted with Ford's approach. Ford chose a Rose Garden strategy, which centered on him staying in the White House so that he
looked presidential. His vice presidential pick, Senator Robert
Dole of Kansas, thus became a pivotal figure in the fall campaign,
standing in for Ford at many of the regional events. During his

kickoff week, Carter scheduled an appearance at the Darlington 500 stock car race. When Carter staffers learned that Dole had also been invited, they negotiated, after some heated exchanges, an agreement whereby Carter would ride in the rear car twice and Dole would ride in the front car once. When Dole was introduced to the crowd, there were some polite cheers. When the announcer introduced Carter, however, the seventy thousand fans in attendance stood up, yelled, cheered, and waved their arms in boisterous support. Dole took his lap around the track and walked up to the VIP booth, where both candidates were supposed to sit. When Carter finished his lap, he unexpectedly walked to the pit to greet people. Then he went into the grandstand to sit with the fans, despite concerns by the Secret Service about his safety. With Dole in the VIP section and Carter with the fans, the event turned into an opportunity to highlight the differences between the parties.[41]

Carter made the most of his come-from-nowhere story. He liked to remind audiences that nobody had expected him to win and that he had risen from obscurity. In some speeches, he said, "I doubt if one percent of this audience ever heard my name a year ago."[42]

Carter was also the first presidential candidate to openly and proudly embrace his evangelical faith. His born-again experience, a story that was repeated in most of the major press coverage about his background, was something that held great appeal to evangelical Protestants and to some fundamentalists, even though the latter were far more conservative on many political issues. Evangelical voters were also a group that, prior to Carter's run, had tended to be apolitical; now it was more likely that they would show up and vote.

Carter refused to take a strong stand on most issues, including the big foreign and domestic policy questions. Opponents continued to say that Carter lacked core values and would say anything to win office. In Carter's mind, however, he sought to move beyond the stalemate of the 1960s. His goal was to appeal ideologically to moderates and independents through a centrist agenda. Defending himself from the accusation that he avoided specific answers, Carter said, "I'm not an ideologue and my positions are not predictable."[43]

Carter struggled to define a new synthesis that could move Democrats beyond the Cold War and the controversial war in Vietnam, a synthesis that included diplomacy, support for human rights in Eastern Europe and elsewhere in the world, and openness in foreign policy making. On domestic policy, Carter's campaign proposals were a hodgepodge of ideas that were difficult to stereotype. He called for tax reform and economic assistance to the unemployed, while promising to balance the budget, reform the welfare system, and streamline government. He supported a pardon of those who evaded the draft. A comprehensive energy policy remained at the top of his agenda alongside expansive environmental regulations. He promised to provide national health care insurance and to curb inflation.

If there was one theme that held Carter's fall campaign together, it was his attack on the political system. Carter's campaign was tailor-made for American politics in the Watergate era. The scandal had rocked confidence in the American political system like almost no other scandal to precede it, certainly within recent memory. This would be the first time since Nixon's downfall that Americans would be going to the polls to elect a president, and Carter's basic campaign message spoke directly to the change in Washington that all Americans sought: "I have been accused of being an outsider. . . . I plead guilty. Unfortunately, the vast majority of Americans are also outsiders. We are not going to get changes by simply shifting around the same groups of insiders, the same tired old rhetoric, the same unkept promises and the same divisive appeals to one party, one faction, one section of the country, one race or religion or one interest group. The insiders have had their chances and they have not delivered. Their time has run out."[44]

Carter was not always comfortable on the campaign trail. In

one event, he spoke at a Los Angeles reception hosted by the actor Warren Beatty. The guests included such prominent figures as Neil Simon, Robert Altman, Sidney Poitier, Hugh Hefner, and more. While many of his staffers were thrilled to hobnob with these stars, Carter didn't think much of the lifestyle. Beatty made the situation tense by joking in his introduction that his friends expected nothing in exchange for their contributions other than nationalizing the oil industry, freeing political prisoners, and other "far-left causes." Carter didn't laugh. He started by saying these were not his objectives, adding that talking to this group would protect him from criticism that he was too pious. When the actor Tony Randall asked Carter if he would support the creation of a federal national theater, Carter said that nobody had ever asked him that question before. When Randall replied, "You've never met with people of this level," Carter coldly responded, "That's why I'm the candidate."[45]

From the start, Pat Caddell was concerned that Carter did not have a solid base of support. Carter had won votes in many states and from numerous social groups, but there was no place where his support was particularly deep, as Caddell had noted on the afternoon of the Massachusetts primary. Approximately one-third of the voters in southern states indicated that they were not very excited about Carter, and he had tenuous support in the Northeast. Traditional groups in the Democratic coalition—women, Catholics, and Jews—were not comfortable with the candidate they intended to vote for. "If I didn't know you were a Democrat," Caddell said to his boss after looking over the numbers, "I'd never be able to tell it from these results."[46] Carter's fall campaign also suffered from mediocre organization.

There were several occasions when Carter's personal mistakes tested the strength of his coalition. One was the September publication of *Playboy*. It was not uncommon in this era for politicians to do interviews or even to write for *Playboy*, which positioned itself as a countercultural magazine, where the articles did matter, in addition to the photographs of nude women. When Carter's interview was first arranged, his staff thought that they would be able to see the final copy and make changes accordingly, just as Jerry Brown had been allowed to do. Most of the interview focused on Carter's ideas about public policy and government. But just as they were leaving the room, with the tape recorder still running, Carter spoke about his feelings regarding religion and tried to explain why he was not as pious as some critics suggested. Carter admitted that he had "committed adultery in my heart many times. This is something that God recognizes I will do—and I have done it—and God forgives me for it. But that doesn't mean that I condemn someone who not only looks on a woman with lust but who leaves his wife and shacks up with somebody out of wedlock." Using language that shocked many readers in September of an election year, Carter also said, "Christ says, don't consider yourself better than someone else because one guy screws a whole bunch of women while the other guy is loyal to his wife." Besides talking about sex, Carter compared President Johnson to Richard Nixon, characterizing both of them as "lying, cheating and distorting the truth."

The article caused a backlash. Many Americans were upset by his comments about lusting after women and the off-color words that he had used. Powell and Jordan watched with dismay as Carter's poll numbers plummeted following the publication of the magazine.[47] Carter's comments contradicted his image of purity, and many Americans wondered whether he was just strange.

Ford was also encountering problems. In addition to governing over a failing economy, the president struggled with the public perception that he was not intelligent and was physically clumsy. Although Ford was one of the most athletic presidents in the nation's history, he had slipped a couple of times and also bumped his head on the door of Air Force One. The popular NBC comedy show *Saturday Night* introduced a sketch where the comedian Chevy Chase portrayed Ford as a president who could not walk five feet without falling all over himself.

Ford hoped to improve his image through three televised debates.

These were the first televised presidential debates since 1960. The first debate was embarrassing for both candidates. With 100 million viewers watching, the microphones stopped working in the middle of the event. Not wanting to make a move that would appear foolish in front of the cameras, Carter and Ford stood still while the cameras remained on. They did this for twenty-seven minutes. "President Ford and I stood there almost like robots," Carter recalled.[48] Once the technicians were finally able to fix the microphones, both men then offered their concluding statements.

The second debate was embarrassing to Ford only. Ford had been overprepared to respond to criticism, which had come from the right wing of his party, about a State Department memo suggesting that the United States should accept the fact that Eastern Europe was under Soviet control. In the debate, Ford had hoped to argue that Eastern Europeans did not consider themselves controlled by the Soviet Union, but it came out differently. When *New York Times* reporter Max Frankel asked Ford about the Soviet issue, the president responded that "there is no Soviet domination of Eastern Europe and there never will be under a Ford Administration." When Frankel, incredulous, followed up, asking Ford to clarify what he meant by his remark, the president made things worse. Carter quickly took advantage of Ford's misstep by saying: "I would like to see Mr. Ford convince the Polish-Americans and the Czech-Americans and the Hungarian-Americans in this country that those countries don't live under the domination and supervision of the Soviet Union behind the Iron Curtain." Backstage after the debate, Caddell told Carter, "That's probably the most decisive presidential debate in history," to which a confident Carter responded, "Wait until you see the next one."[49]

By the end of October, the polls showed a statistical dead heat. This was stunning—evidence that Caddell's continued warnings about the soft vote were right on target—given that Carter had been up by about 30 percent after the convention and nothing particularly good happened in October with Ford in charge.

. . .

In November, Carter won, but by one of the narrowest margins in U.S. history. Democrats gained control of the White House and Congress for the first time since 1968. But the Democratic coalition was fragile. Carter received 50.1 percent of the popular vote and 297 electoral votes to Ford's 48 percent of the popular vote and 240 electoral votes (Reagan received 1 electoral vote). Turnout was the lowest since 1948. Democrats retained control of Congress with an influx of younger, suburban-based Democrats who were not tied to older Democratic ideas. The Senate Democratic majority rose from 60 to 61, and in the House from 291 to 292.[50]

Carter's victory was regional. Eighty percent of his Electoral College support was from the Northeast and South.[51] He did well in northern industrial states, although he often pulled his strongest support from suburban rather than the traditional urban areas. His support among African Americans and Jewish voters was good although not exceptionally high. He did poorly with some traditional Democratic voters such as Catholics.[52] The lack of support from these core Democratic constituencies did not bode well since their representatives dominated the Democratic leadership in Congress.

Still, the coalition held together, and, indeed, Carter had depended on them for his victory. In fact, Carter won as a result of the very Democratic loyalists and machines that he had criticized. The Democratic National Committee was instrumental to his turnout and organized labor came out in full force. Middle- and lower-income Americans, the heart of the New Deal coalition, were central to his victory.[53] Carter's skillful campaigning and party support had squeaked him into office. Now he needed to ensure that the fragile center held.

4

A Year of Promise

Carter brings a distinctly different personality,
heritage, focus and set of goals to the presidency than
did his predecessors. He promised change in his
campaign—and he promised one thing more: personal
accountability for bringing it to pass.

—David S. Broder (1977)

In December 1976, Carter met with Texas congressman Jack
Brooks, chairman of the House Committee on Government Operations, and told the congressman that he intended to seek authority
to reorganize the federal government for greater efficiency. The
legislation Carter was proposing was not new; it had passed for
presidents several times since Harry Truman. In 1973, however,
Congress balked and refused to extend the measure. Capitol Hill
was tired of President Nixon's continual efforts to circumvent the
legislative process and was thus opposed to any extension of executive power. The president-elect wanted the authority back, and
he justified the request with a post-Watergate argument. He
wanted to combine and cut federal agencies, reduce the number
of civil servants, and deregulate certain areas of policy because, he

argued, most people found the federal bureaucracy too complex, too remote, and too intrusive.

Brooks was not pleased with Carter's proposal. The chairman repeatedly interrupted Carter to say that government would be reorganized according to the vision of Congress, not the president. Pulling out records that he had collected from the 1960s, Brooks said, "Governor, Lyndon Johnson was the greatest arm-twister Washington has ever seen, and he did not like to get beat on Capitol Hill. Look at this list! He was never successful in getting more than one-third of his proposed reorganization plans through Congress, even with this special procedure. If you win this argument on the legislation, you still won't have anything to show for it." Carter replied that he had "promised the American people" so he could not put this aside.[1] The discussion disintegrated so badly that adviser Bert Lance felt the need to step in to move the conversation on to a different subject.[2]

Carter didn't forget the encounter, nor did he back down. On January 7, Carter met with the new Speaker of the House, Tip O'Neill from Massachusetts, and the new majority leader, James Wright of Texas, to tell them that if any committee chair stalled his reorganization proposals he would use every ounce of his power to move bills around them. He singled out Congressman Brooks. According to Wright, O'Neill looked like Carter had just given him "strychnine on the rocks." Without hesitation, the Speaker responded, "That would be the worst thing you could do, Mr. President. . . . Particularly with a fellow like Brooks. Jack doesn't get mad; he gets even. You don't know your throat is cut until you try to turn your head."[3]

But Carter couldn't help himself. In stark contrast to previous Democratic presidents like Lyndon Johnson, he simply did not like legislative politics. His discomfort caused even more tension than it might have under different circumstances. The congressional leadership didn't particularly trust Carter any more than he did them and didn't feel that they shared political interests. Also, Carter took office after the brutal battles between Nixon and the

Democratic Congress in which legislators had passed a series of reforms—such as the War Powers Act of 1973 and the Budget Reform Act of 1974—aimed at taking power away from the president and giving it back to the legislative branch. Still bruised by Nixon, Congress was in no mood to hand over the reins to an incoming president they barely knew.

For his part, Carter wasn't bothered by the reaction from Brooks or O'Neill. The president wanted to govern without being beholden to established political leaders and was determined to plunge ahead. The day after the inauguration, Carter made a dramatic decision that reflected his desire, regardless of the political costs, to end the divisiveness of the Vietnam era. In his first executive order, the president gave Vietnam War draft evaders an unconditional pardon, forgiving thousands already convicted, under indictment, or who had fled abroad without registering for the draft. Many veterans' organizations were unhappy with President Carter's decision. An official from the Veterans of Foreign Wars said, "We feel that there is a better way for people who have broken laws to come back into the country, and that's through one of the pillars of the formation of our nation—and that is our present system of justice."[4] But fulfilling the campaign pledge was important to Carter, who believed that the controversies that grew out of the 1960s, like Vietnam, were holding back the nation.

. . .

Carter ran as the consummate outsider, but his White House team offered a more complex picture of how he would govern. Carter combined Georgia loyalists, policy experts, and Washington insiders. Hamilton Jordan served as assistant to the president, a position Carter used as an alternative to having a chief of staff, while Charles Kirbo informally offered counsel. Carter centralized decision making around himself while leaving his advisers in a constant state of competition for his attention (called the "spokes of the wheel" style of advising). Jody Powell worked as press secretary. Stuart Eizenstat was responsible for domestic policy. Bert

Lance headed the Office of Management and Budget. Although presidents since Franklin Roosevelt had relied on pollsters, Carter elevated the twenty-six-year-old Pat Caddell, known among colleagues as the most pessimistic man in the business, to a higher stature by seeking his guidance on almost every initiative.[5]

Not everyone in the White House was part of the "Georgia Mafia," however. Well-established policy experts such as National Security Adviser Zbigniew Brzezinski, a Columbia University professor of international relations whom Carter had met on the Trilateral Commission, were brought into the White House. And notwithstanding Carter's antiestablishment persona, a surprising number of his appointments went to Washington insiders. James Schlesinger, secretary of defense under Presidents Nixon and Ford, worked as the first secretary of energy. Nobody was more of a Washington insider than the new secretary of state, Cyrus Vance, a Yale-educated Wall Street lawyer who had worked as deputy secretary of defense under Robert McNamara. Vance, a well-known figure throughout the foreign policy bureaucracy, had the look and feel of one of the characters in David Halberstam's classic work *The Best and the Brightest*. Secretary of Health, Education and Welfare (HEW) Joseph Califano was a prominent Democrat who had been responsible for domestic policy under President Johnson, and another Johnson veteran, economist Charles Schultze, chaired the Council of Economic Advisers. Harold Brown, the new secretary of defense, had also worked under Johnson, first as the U.S. deputy defense secretary and then as secretary of the air force.

One of his most controversial picks was Griffin Bell to be attorney general. Charles Kirbo, one of his law partners, had strongly recommended Bell for the position. Many observers were surprised by the pick since Bell, who was a member of white-only clubs, had been a key political player on Carter's campaign and as a federal judge had been slow to achieve school integration. During Bell's confirmation hearings, Senator Strom Thurmond, a remnant of the Old South, spoke very well of the nominee—a kiss of death

in the minds of liberals. Carter tried to temper some of the disappointment among civil rights activists by appointing the civil
rights lawyer Drew Days to direct the Civil Rights Division of the
Department of Justice.[6]

• • •

During their first months, Caddell kept advising the president
that symbolic actions should be a serious part of the White House
portfolio given that Carter's election victory was so narrow and
since so many Americans still had only a vague sense of what the
new president stood for.[7] The president instructed the Marines
Corps band to stop playing "Hail to the Chief" whenever he
entered a room. And in another sign that he wanted no truck with
the more ostentatious aspects of the presidency, Carter sold the
presidential yacht, the *Sequoia*. One frustrated Republican com-
mented, "He was folks, and folks is in."[8] Carter had even gone
down to the White House mess hall for lunch to eat a cheese-
burger and iced tea with the staff. As when he was governor,
Carter conducted town meetings around the country, sometimes
staying overnight at the home of regular citizens.[9]

Symbols, however, could go only so far. Difficult—and poten-
tially controversial—actions would also need to be taken if Carter
wanted to fulfill his hope of transcending the traditional policy
options that had been offered to Americans over the past few
decades. The administration believed that in order to establish
the political conditions for negotiations with the Soviets over
arms control (building on the Strategic Arms Limitation Talks
[SALT I], a treaty signed by Nixon in 1972), Carter would have
to demonstrate a willingness to pressure the Soviet Union and
denounce its human rights violations. As Jody Powell wrote the
president in February, "One of the reasons Ford-Kissinger failed . . .
was because the American people would not support a policy which
seemed to abandon our position in support of human rights."[10]

Determined to follow through on his promise to achieve such
a balance, in February the president, after receiving a letter from

the dissident intellectual Andrei Sakharov detailing human rights abuses in the Soviet Union, responded with a letter in which Carter expressed his support for Sakharov and the struggle for human rights.[11] Leonid Brezhnev's response, on February 25, reflected his clear displeasure with Carter's approach. According to Bert Lance, Carter "didn't care whether other folks and other world figures agreed or disagreed. As far as he was concerned, anyone who disagreed was simply wrong."[12]

Carter's early interaction with congressional Democrats did not go much better than his discussions with the Soviets. The situation on Capitol Hill would have been difficult for any president regardless of how well, or badly, they interacted with legislators. Congressional reforms in the 1970s had fragmented power in the institution, elections had filled both houses with newcomers who were not beholden to the leadership, and fewer members were willing to unite for the good of the party alone. Hamilton Jordan said that "we . . . had no unifying Democratic consensus, no program, no set of principles on which a majority of Democrats agreed."[13]

The president's congressional staff did not help the situation. Frank Moore, the congressional liaison, had limited experience on Capitol Hill and made some embarrassing blunders. For example, one legislator was infuriated when he had to hear the news on the radio that the president was visiting his district. At one breakfast meeting hosted by the president, only sweet rolls were served instead of the usual full breakfast. Speaker O'Neill yelled at Vice President Mondale, "I didn't get this way eating sweet rolls. I want a breakfast and I'm not coming back unless I get a meal!"[14] O'Neill, an irrepressible Irish-Catholic Bostonian who believed that "all politics is local," felt that there was a fundamental divide, even in the new generation, between Democrats from his region and southerners. Carter's team, O'Neill said, "just didn't understand Irish or Jewish politicians, or the nuances of city politics." He characterized a southern politician as a "sweet talker who can skin you alive with his charm" in contrast to a northern legislator who is "far more blunt and rambunctious."[15]

Among Carter's most controversial decisions in February was his attempt to oppose some of the proposals for funding over three hundred water projects across the country that President Ford had included in his final budget. Carter dismissed the proposals as congressional pork. He sent a letter to Congress stating that nineteen of the projects would be cut. Congress was furious. These funds were essential to their constituents. Those affected by Carter's list included Senator Russell Long, the powerful chair of the Senate Finance Committee. The Senate overturned most of Carter's decisions.[16]

. . .

Having a lukewarm, sometimes hostile, relationship with the Democratic political establishment also had its benefits. Because of his tenuous standing in the party, Carter, whose public approval ratings reached 75 percent in April, felt more freedom to tackle big, complex issues that party officials had been inclined to avoid because they threatened key interests or did not promise clear-cut electoral rewards.

In fact, Carter was sometimes able to obtain what he wanted precisely because he did not feel beholden to congressional power-houses. The reorganization plan that Brooks and Speaker O'Neill rebuffed in Carter's earliest days provides a dramatic example. After his encounter with Brooks, Carter reached out to Republicans, who were more favorably disposed to the plan from the start as it promised to reduce "big government." Carter then used the Republican votes he had in hand to build pressure on Democrats. Democrats, afraid of looking bad as the opponents of efficient government, moved closer to Carter's position. Just one month after the election, Congress passed the measure by large margins in the House and the Senate. Even Brooks went along with the bill after one minor concession to placate him. By standing firm, Carter had received the authority he sought.

Whereas many presidents vow to tackle the biggest challenges of the day but then back off as soon as they take office, Carter was determined to keep his promise to act as a transformative leader in his first hundred days. His most ambitious objective was to tackle the nation's energy crisis. In 1973, following the Arab-Israeli war, members of the Organization of the Petroleum Exporting Countries (OPEC) imposed an oil embargo on the United States. Although the embargo had ended in 1974, America's consumption of oil remained a central political issue. Carter believed that the energy crisis would only be resolved when the government formulated programs to reduce energy consumption and end the nation's dependence on the Middle East. When the price of gasoline increased after the embargo of 1973–74, the government under President Nixon had relied on voluntary rations and caps on sales. These solutions, including Ford's program to remove price controls, were not working in the short term, though. While some Americans began to purchase smaller cars, and Congress, in 1974, established a fifty-five-mile-per-hour speed limit, the primary response of the nation had been to accept higher prices rather than reduce their consumption of fuel.

James Schlesinger chaired the task force charged with developing an energy conservation proposal, an assignment filled with minefields. A comprehensive plan was certain to anger many different parts of the Democratic coalition. Higher prices were needed to dissuade consumers from excessive consumption, but this would not sit well with northeastern Democrats, who had just suffered through a cold, snowy winter with high fuel costs. At the same time, southern Democrats from oil-producing states firmly opposed further regulations on production. Adding to the challenge was the fact that the political pressure for reform had diminished because oil prices decreased for consumers between 1974 and 1978.[17]

Schlesinger's team worked in total secrecy based on the justification that this was the only way to design a policy proposal without being stifled by the divisions among Democrats. They were given ninety days to finish the plan. Carter "thinks people work better with a gun at their heads," according to one White House aide.[18]

On April 18, 1977, Carter announced that he would propose a

national energy program to reduce American dependence on oil-producing countries. In a televised address, modeled on FDR's fireside chats, Carter explained that the energy crisis demanded sacrifices that would be "painful" for Americans. This challenge, the president said, was " 'the moral equivalent of war,' except that we will be uniting our efforts to build and not to destroy." Carter implored Americans to change their consumption patterns and called for manufacturing regulations to encourage energy-efficient appliances. "Tonight I want to have an unpleasant talk with you about a problem unprecedented in our history. With the exception of preventing war, this is the greatest challenge our country will face during our lifetimes. The energy crisis has not yet overwhelmed us, but it will if we do not act quickly," the president said. Carter felt that it was intolerable that the United States imported 36 percent of its oil from Arab countries since it made the nation vulnerable to "political blackmail."[19]

His advisers warned that the failure to handle the energy crisis successfully would mean failure in other areas.[20] The National Energy Plan (NEP), as it was called, was a complicated measure that included over one hundred provisions. The proposal included the centralization of policy planning, stronger regulations on energy production, taxes on gas-guzzling cars, federal money for energy research, tax credits for home insulation, and more. The NEP maintained the oil industry's existing regulatory structure while loosening key areas to allow the government to begin slowing down energy consumption. As the House started to consider the bill, it became clear that passage, if it came, would take months.

At the same time that Carter put forward his energy plan, he made human rights the centerpiece of his foreign policy. "Our commitment to human rights must be absolute," the president said in his inaugural address. Carter wanted the nation to employ its military and moral strength to ease Cold War tensions and curtail social injustice across the globe. Human rights, he believed, offered an ideological framework that seemed to have disappeared from American foreign policy when the war in Vietnam undermined faith in the policy of containment. "Our country has been strongest and most effective," Carter later argued in his memoirs, "when morality and a commitment to freedom and democracy have been most clearly emphasized in our foreign policy."[21]

Many presidents had spoken about human rights, but Carter actually took a series of steps to institutionalize this policy. His administration established a Bureau of Human Rights and Humanitarian Affairs in the State Department. He appointed as the first coordinator Patricia Derian, who then became assistant secretary of state for Human Rights and Humanitarian Affairs. Derian had cut her teeth on the civil rights movement, participating in grassroots organizing and mobilizing in Mississippi in the 1960s, and like many advocates she perceived human rights as a natural extension of the civil rights agenda. The State Department also began to release an annual human rights report that graded each country on how it treated its citizens.

Dramatic moves in foreign policy were also needed, Carter believed, because of the widespread problems confronting America in the post-Vietnam era. Confidence in the United States as a leading superpower had eroded. OPEC nations appeared to be holding the country hostage; the U.S. economy seemed incapable of recovery just as West Germany and Japan were emerging as economic powerhouses; and Soviet expansionism in areas such as Africa belied the notion that the threats of the Cold War had ended. Carter set out to shake up international policy.

Carter and his advisers also sensed that human rights could be a good political issue given the divisions within the Democratic Party between neoconservative hawks and liberal doves. On the one hand, neoconservatives such as Senator Scoop Jackson, greatly concerned about the plight of Soviet Jewry, argued that the United States should refuse to negotiate with the Soviet Union until the Kremlin demonstrated a commitment to human rights. On the other hand, human rights supporters on the Democratic left, including Donald Fraser of Minnesota and Tom Harkin of Iowa, called for a foreign policy less strictly focused on anticommunism and more concerned with recognizing the political rights of oppressed groups. Harkin and Fraser's vision, a fundamental reorientation, meant adopting a critical perspective toward authoritarian Cold War allies as well as supporting rebel groups that might lean toward socialism as long as their primary concern was obtaining human rights for oppressed minorities.

Carter tried to emphasize the pragmatic middle, balancing his calls for the Soviets to respect human rights with equally strong support for working out the SALT II accord that would follow up on the arms agreements that Nixon had struck with the Soviets in 1972. Carter justified the negotiations with the Soviets, telling Americans that they needed to overcome the "inordinate fear of communism" that led the United States into bad policy decisions.

The administration's focus on practical ways to gain recognition for minorities meant that it was not always consistent in how it implemented human rights policy. In dealing with South Africa, Carter backed away from proposals for economic sanctions and divestment, instead settling for promoting foreign investment as a way to improve the lives of blacks. This was the type of pragmatic turn that left many liberal human rights proponents frustrated.[22]

Carter's most ambitious foreign policy initiative was to try to achieve a peace agreement in the Middle East. Besides the immense challenge of bringing peace to this tension-filled region of the world, just taking on this issue would be politically difficult for Carter given the tensions that existed between him and American Jewish voters, a loyal Democratic constituency. A majority of Jewish voters supported Carter in the 1976 election although they were nervous about his evangelical Christian identity, his lukewarm record on civil rights while in Georgia, and rumors that he would not be sympathetic toward Israel with regard to Palestinian claims over the West Bank.

The political dangers, however, did not deter the president. Carter made a comprehensive Middle East peace agreement a top priority. Such an agreement, he said, referencing the bloody Arab-Israeli battles of 1967 and 1973, would be the only way to prevent further wars involving Israel. Carter also stressed a multilateral approach, explaining that "since I had made our nation's commitment to human rights a central tenet of our foreign policy, it was impossible for me to ignore the very serious problems on the West Bank."[23]

Carter's team realized that mobilizing domestic approval for such an agreement would be essential. Jordan produced a lengthy strategic memo for the president in which he explained how the Jewish community had achieved so much political power despite the fact that they constituted only about 3 percent of the population. The first factor behind their influence, Jordan argued, was that Jews registered and voted at much higher levels than the rest of the population. The second factor, Jordan wrote, was that Jewish voters made generous financial contributions to candidates who supported their causes. Third, American Jews had achieved a remarkable degree of organizational effectiveness as a lobby. AIPAC (American Israel Public Affairs Committee) could count on somewhere between sixty-five and seventy-five votes in the Senate alone. Finally, and most important, Jordan said that Jews pursued their defense of Israel in a "vacuum" since "there does not exist in this country a political counterforce that opposes the specific goals of the Jewish lobby."[24]

Well aware of the need to drum up support among American Jewish voters and their organizations for the administration's plans, Carter's staff established a lobby to this end. Mark Siegel and Edward Sanders (former director of AIPAC) handled these responsibilities. Sanders arranged for administration speakers to meet with the Jewish community, scheduled appointments for Jewish leaders to meet with White House officials, sent mailings to key organizations and handled personal correspondence, and arranged for spokesmen to deliver speeches at synagogues and community institutions.[25]

Senior congressional Democrats warned Carter that he should avoid the issue of peace in the Middle East, saying that it was a "losing proposition."[26] Carter's first meeting with Israeli leaders, which had taken place in March, was disastrous. Carter had no personal chemistry with Prime Minister Yitzhak Rabin. In his diary, Carter noted that he found Rabin to be "very timid, very stubborn, and also somewhat ill at ease."[27] Carter wrote that Rabin displayed the same intransigence when it was just the two of them in a room as when they were in public. Rabin was equally put off by Carter's approach, and the Israeli leadership left the White House meeting sensing that they were no longer a priority for the president.

Carter's determination to pursue peace in the Middle East had the potential to get him into political hot water domestically, especially if he was going to choose a path of working closely with Arab nations that were not traditionally perceived as strong allies of the United States. In the first few months of his presidency, Carter had met with Arab leaders from Jordan, Syria, Saudi Arabia, and Egypt. Relations with Jewish voters remained extremely tense. When Carter officials met with Jewish leaders in September to talk about the situation in Israel, the leaders warned that American Jews were worried that President Carter would blame the Israelis for a failure to achieve a peace agreement, and they felt that the president was "less than evenhanded" in his treatment of Israel, criticizing West Bank settlements while remaining silent on the actions of the PLO (Palestine Liberation Organization). In general, they said, the administration had developed "an image of insensitivity toward Jewish concerns for Israel" within the community.[28]

• • •

While Carter outlined his ambitions for energy and human rights policies, including Middle East peace, the Democratic Congress was far more interested in alleviating the impact of stagflation on their constituents. High rates of unemployment and inflation were hitting voters from both ends, and representatives were feeling the anger of the electorate.

When Carter turned to bread-and-butter pocketbook issues, he lived up to his campaign trail promise to independent voters that he would not be beholden to core Democratic interest groups, including organized labor and their Democratic supporters, whom he saw as being as much a part of the political establishment as many corporate forces. Carter's economic stimulus bill proved an occasion to hold the line. The stimulus legislation, aimed at fulfilling Carter's promise to prioritize lowering the unemployment rate, included a fifty-dollar tax rebate, in addition to public spending and tax cuts for lower- and middle-income Americans. Carter agreed with West Virginia's senator Robert Byrd and the fiscal hawks that the rebate would be too costly and that it would never have any impact. When the economy showed slight signs of improvement, Carter used it as a reason to pull the provision. The unions, who saw the rebate as the only legislative piece that would benefit working- and middle-class Americans (though they felt it was much too meager), were furious. Congressional Democrats were also greatly displeased; they had fought for the rebate only to be left standing before angry constituents with empty hands.[29] The final legislation, which passed Congress in May, contained the proposed tax cuts, and provided financial assistance to state and local governments, but included only a modest jobs program. Despite the pressure coming from congressional Democrats to do more to create jobs, Carter held firm on spending.

Carter insisted on being frugal with the budget, even if it aggravated core supporters such as African American legislators. The president, who had created the Urban and Regional Policy Group to study urban reform, revealed that he would not commit to bold measures to transform U.S. cities. He told his advisers, "Don't tell me we'll spend more money all around, then we'll call it an urban policy. Give me something worth funding if you want more money."[30]

Overall, however, party optimism remained high in the summer of 1977. Democrats controlled the White House and Congress, the president had been able to move forward with a number of initiatives in his first hundred days, and his approval ratings remained very strong. "He stands extraordinarily high in personal popularity and general approval polls," wrote *Washington Post* columnist Joseph Kraft in May. "Republicans and Independents like him as well as Democrats do. He appeals to both Southern blacks and the followers of George Wallace. Moreover, as the pollster Peter Hart has shown, Carter has built as president something he never had during the campaign, and that both Ford and Nixon lacked: a large number of voters strongly attached to his leadership, 'a sizable core constituency.' "[31]

For this reason, congressional Democrats were willing to take risks for the new president. The administration's energy plan had been debated in the House following the April speech. The numerous divisions among Democrats over the measure made it difficult. To make matters more challenging, the legislation was subject to the control of over five committees and numerous subcommittees. "When I declared the energy effort to be the moral equivalent of war," Carter said, "it was impossible for me to imagine the bloody legislative battles we would have to win before the major campaign was over."[32]

When Speaker O'Neill watched the debates over the complex five-volume proposal and the number of people handling the bill, he knew right away it spelled trouble. Despite his uneasy relationship with Carter, O'Neill decided to save the president's bill by using the powers of the speakership that had been produced by congressional reform in the early 1970s. The Speaker assembled an ad hoc committee to handle the legislation and, as a result of O'Neill's efforts and leadership, the energy measure passed the House relatively intact in August 1977.

. . .

Ironically, an ethics scandal caused the administration its greatest political problem. Office of Management and Budget director Bert Lance's investments from his days as the president of the Calhoun National Bank of Georgia became a subject of Senate investigation in the summer when Carter was working on human rights, energy, and an economic stimulus. During his confirmation hearings earlier in the year, Lance had promised that he would sell his stocks in Georgia banks before having to deal with any legislation related to banking. In the early summer, Lance discovered that selling his stock in the downturn would be a huge financial blow to himself and to the banks. He had asked the president if he could place the stock in a blind trust so there would be no charges of impropriety and so the stock could be sold under better market conditions. As the Senate Governmental Affairs Committee considered the change, questions emerged in the press about alleged financial improprieties during Lance's time in Georgia, including a $3.4 million loan he received from the First National Bank of Chicago. The Senate had not found anything wrong in its investigation and approved Lance's request. An investigation by the Comptroller of the Currency found Lance did nothing legally wrong, though some investigators said he had shown poor judgment on "unsound" practices.

At a press conference in August, following the release of the Comptroller reporter, Carter turned to Lance and said, "Bert, I'm proud of you." Many advisers thought Carter needed to get rid of Lance. They argued that the president had campaigned on the issue of trust so that Lance's mere presence in the administration was a political problem. Carter had promised to uphold the highest ethical standards in presidential history and said that his administration would not even give the appearance of impropriety. The president refused however to abandon his friend. The press was another matter. Their attention remained fixed on the scandal. "It wasn't self-paralysis," one aide explained. "It was just that every time we would try to talk about other issues, we would be asked, but what about Bert Lance? We'd try to lobby stuff on the Hill. Frank Moore's people would go see senators and congressmen. Moore's staff would try to talk about the votes on the bill, and be asked what is the president going to do about Bert Lance? We ended up being paralyzed by it."[33]

In this context, Carter's defiant stand did not sit well. Carter refused to back down. The post-Watergate media entered a feeding frenzy about the story. The newspapers were consumed by stories about Lance throughout August as well as for much of September.[34] In the middle of September, Lance appeared again before a Senate committee and more accusations emerged, including the claim that some in his wife's family had written bad checks without consequences. *Time* magazine concluded, "It was inevitable, of course, that the old memories of Johnson and Nixon surfaced. Though Carter's troubles were only a tiny fraction of those of the other two Presidents, the pattern of response was distressingly familiar."[35]

Lance finally resigned on September 21, when it became clear the kind of damage that was being done. Although Lance would later be acquitted of wrongdoing in a trial following his resignation, Carter's presidency was never the same. "It is impossible to overestimate the damage inflicted on my administration by charges leveled against Bert Lance," Carter said.[36]

• • •

As Carter tried to recover from the damage of the Lance scandal in the fall, he completed negotiations with General Omar Torrijos Herrera, the leader of the Panamanian government, regarding a treaty that would return control of the Panama Canal to Panama. The proposal was part of Carter's effort to cool the tensions that had emerged in regions such as Central America and to show smaller nations that the United States could act as something other than a superpower. Carter believed that General Torrijos faced a possible revolution that would bring instability to this region. Additionally, the administration thought that Torrijos was a leader who could work with the United States.[37]

It was a risky proposal. "The only people who give a damn are the ones who oppose it," one White House staffer said.[38] The Department of State's deputy spokesperson Jill Schuker had written Carter in June 1977 that the public generally thought that "we are giving away the [Panama] Canal—giving up what is 'rightfully ours.'" The First Lady warned the president that he should wait until his second term to make such a controversial decision, but her warning "fell on deaf ears."[39]

The president and General Torrijos signed two treaties on September 7. The treaties, Carter said at the signing ceremony, "mark the commitment of the United States to the belief that fairness, and not force, should lie at the heart of our dealings with the nations of the world." With conservative organizations preparing to make the Panama treaties a focus of their attacks on the president, Carter understood that he would incur a high price for persuading the Senate to ratify them.[40]

· · ·

Carter made progress with his initiatives, but he also had to deal with the realities of congressional politics. The proposals that presidents send to Congress do not always come out in the form that the White House is hoping for. The Senate passed Carter's energy legislation in October, though with most of the provisions in the original proposal stripped away. Majority Leader Robert Byrd had not been as accommodating as O'Neill, allowing various committees to handle the legislation and thus giving opponents ample opportunities to undermine it. When the Senate finally voted in support of a bill, key provisions such as a tax on gas-guzzling automobiles had been abandoned. "I'm just wondering," Senator Abraham Ribicoff of Connecticut said, "if the President shouldn't admit that his energy program is a shambles."[41] The bill then stalled in conference committee until October 1978.

There were also missteps. In the middle of the administration's concerted effort to court Jewish voters for Carter's Middle East peace initiative, the United States and the Soviets issued a joint communiqué in October 1977 that called for a Geneva conference at which a plan for peace could be discussed. The Soviet-U.S. communiqué, which Carter officials had thought would be a landmark achievement and a first step toward a diplomatic meeting by separating the issue from the Cold War, was also the first time that the United States had publicly mentioned the "official rights" of Palestinians. Jewish leaders had not been given advance warning of the communiqué, and adviser Mark Siegel reported that as a result

Carter's "stock in the American Jewish community" had fallen below "any U.S. President since the creation of the State of Israel." Siegel implored Hamilton Jordan to quickly improve their public outreach campaign with Jewish voters and organizations.[42]

• • •

The first year of Carter's presidency concluded with several break-throughs overseas and at home, some of which were not of Carter's own doing but which confirmed the arguments he was making. Following several failed attempts to arrange a conference in Geneva, Egyptian president Anwar Sadat decided to travel to Israel on a historic visit and made a surprise speech in Israel's legislative branch, the Knesset, on November 20. Sadat was the kind of cosmopolitan leader that U.S. officials had not previously encountered. He was Western in his dress and bold in his ambition, sending signals that he was willing to make moves that would anger other Arab leaders. Sadat was also struggling with political problems back home, including a terrible economy and the growing threat of the Muslim Brotherhood. Sadat's speech in Israel centered on the need for peace, and he called for a solution to the status of the occupied territories. This was the first time that a leading Arab had visited Israel. Impressed by the speech, Menachem Begin, the tough, hard-line conservative Likud Party leader who had become prime minister of Israel in May, concluded that discussions with Egypt would be beneficial. By limiting negotiations to one Arab country, Israel could contain the number of demands that were made on it.[43]

The following month, Carter enjoyed one of the biggest legislative accomplishments of his presidency: the Social Security Amendments of 1977, which raised additional taxes and reduced benefits by correcting a technical error made in 1972. The House voted for the legislation by 189 to 163 and the Senate 56 to 21. There were 109 Republicans in the House who opposed the bill, with conservative opponents calling this the largest peacetime "tax increase" in American history. The legislation, which the president signed into law on December 20, resolved the short-term solvency crisis.

Within his first year as president, Carter had launched an ambitious human rights program, started negotiations for a peace agreement in the Middle East, and made progress on a number of domestic programs, including Social Security and an economic stimulus bill. He had had his tensions with Congress, Democrats, and the Soviet Union, but the problems in no way overwhelmed him. After running a campaign promising change and independence, he had kept his promises and governed this way even though there had been political costs to doing so. His polls had climbed back up to 54 percent in a Gallup Poll conducted in November (although the number who "strongly" approved had fallen from 42 percent in March to 19 percent).[44] The fall months had been rough, but Carter was going into his second year with the potential to build a successful presidency.

On December 31, Carter spent New Year's Eve in Tehran with the shah of Iran. Despite Carter's quest for human rights and concerns about the activities of the shah's secret police, Carter defended the United States's economic and military support for the Iranian government. The shah and Carter had enjoyed a productive meeting the previous month in Washington, notwithstanding unexpectedly intense protests outside the White House (the tear gas that police used to break up the protest wafted onto the White House lawn and caused the officials there to cough and wipe their eyes with handkerchiefs as the president spoke).

"Iran, because of the great leadership of the Shah, is an island of stability in one of the more troubled areas of the world," Carter enthusiastically said during his toast to the shah at the New Year's celebration. That toast would come back to haunt him. As the two leaders drove to the airport, Carter saw the other reality in Iran. Outside the window, young men threw rocks at their car and yelled "Allahu Akbar."[45]

5

Conservatives Rising, Democrats Dividing

He owes us the presidency and always has. If you like
your president and want to keep him, you'd better
knock some sense into his head about a program of full
employment, housing and national health insurance.

—Congressman John Conyers (1978)

Jimmy Carter remained optimistic about the future of his presidency when he delivered his State of the Union address in January 1978. "For the first time in a generation," the president said to Congress as he made several proposals, including the creation of a Department of Education as well as a tax cut, "we are not haunted by a major international crisis or by domestic turmoil; and we now have a rare and priceless opportunity to address persistent problems and burdens which come to us as a nation quietly and are steadily getting worse over the years." The president's top priorities were to continue pressuring the House and Senate to complete their deliberations over the energy package as well as for the Senate to ratify the Panama Canal treaties.

Faced with the challenges that he encountered the previous fall, which started with the Bert Lance scandal, Carter was determined to work even harder to move his agenda forward. With his approval ratings declining, Carter became obsessed with getting a handle on legislation. He began to read hundreds of pages of memoranda and policy analysis every single night before going to sleep. "You badly need rest and the opportunity to rejuvenate," Hamilton Jordan wrote Carter in February. "You don't look good."[1]

With Carter's approval ratings down to 34 percent in February, conservative activists and politicians sensed an opportunity to strengthen their political position against the president and to improve their numbers in Washington. While there had been a right wing within American politics since the end of World War II, a full-scale conservative movement—connecting grassroots activism to Washington-based think tanks and lobbying organizations— had taken hold only in the 1970s. The New Right was now busy constructing a powerful organizational infrastructure: political action committees, volunteer operations, radio talk shows, think tanks, and a direct-mail network.

During the spring of 1978, the Panama Canal treaties emerged as the focus of conservative attack against Carter and the Democratic Party. Some conservative activists and politicians argued that since its opening in 1914 the canal had symbolized American power overseas. Giving the canal back to the Panamanians would reflect a reversal of America's influence in the aftermath of Vietnam. Conservatives were also concerned that the Soviets were attempting to expand their power in Central America and that any removal of American influence in the region posed a practical danger. The leadership of organizations such as the American Conservative Union, the Conservative Caucus, and the Committee for the Survival of a Free Congress coordinated their campaign against the treaties through the umbrella organizations of the Committee to Save the Panama Canal and the Emergency Coalition to Save the Panama Canal.[2] The groups paid for prominent speakers to travel across the country and warn about the dangers that would ensue if the Senate ratified the treaties. The American Conservative Union produced fake television "documentaries" that urged viewers to send letters to their representatives.[3] Conservative Republicans also publicized their message about foreign policy through the floor debates in the Senate.

At this critical point in his presidency, Carter made a decision to focus most of his energy on the ratification of the treaties, while putting other issues aside. "It's hard to concentrate on anything except Panama," Carter noted in his diary.[4] Since Carter could not match the grassroots strength of the conservative movement, the president personally lobbied senators and appealed directly to the citizen groups. Throughout the spring, senators were blitzed with fact sheets from the White House about why the treaties were important. Carter also turned to horse trading and ego stroking with senators. When push came to shove, Carter showed that he was capable of legislative politicking even though it was an aspect of politics he intensely disliked. Carter flew several contingents of senators to Panama so that they could see the canal for themselves and be briefed by military leaders, local residents, and business leaders.[5] The president said, "I'll stand by the door and if you would like to come and have a picture made, fine."[6] Carter addressed audiences in local communities around the country through state-of-the-art "town meetings" that relied on remote telephone connections.[7] Finally, Carter attempted to exploit divisions that existed within the Republican Party. Barry Goldwater, Gerald Ford, William Buckley, and John Wayne publicly stated that the treaties did not pose any strategic threat and that winning over public opinion in Latin America was important to combat Soviet and Cuban influence.

The tactics were enough for Carter to win the battle over the treaties. The Panamanians would control the canal starting in 2000. In the final Senate debates, the administration was forced to concede a key provision that authorized the United States to intervene militarily if necessary to keep the canal open. In March 1978, the Senate ratified the first treaty by a one-vote margin (68 to 32, with two-thirds of the Senate needed for ratification) and ratified the second treaty in April 1978 (68 to 32). The treaties gradually shifted control over the canal to Panama and proclaimed that the canal was neutral territory. The media started to speak of a "new Carter" who was more shrewd and savvy than the politician who had sometimes stumbled throughout his first year in the White House.[8]

But Carter chose to demonstrate his legislative skills in a politically costly battle, one that did not make him or his party politically stronger. The ratification of the Panama treaties did not win over any important friends or forge any blocs of support for the White House at home, and it actually strengthened Carter's opponents. While conservatives lost the ratification debate, they exited the Senate battle with renewed energy at the grassroots level and with greater organizational strength. Meanwhile, Carter had expended a great deal of political capital, including with Republican moderates like Senate Minority Leader Howard Baker who were not very keen on the treaties and who didn't want to make more deals with the president.[9]

Meanwhile, tensions flared over the Middle East. In March 1978, the Palestine Liberation Organization had launched a brutal terrorist attack in Tel Aviv that resulted in the death of thirty-eight Israelis. The Israelis responded by attacking PLO outposts in Lebanon, using cluster bombs that had been made in the United States, a move that Carter believed to be too severe. Carter went so far as to threaten to challenge Israel's trade status with the United States.[10]

The combination of human rights and détente proved difficult to sustain in the summer of 1978. When President Carter engaged in discussions with the Soviet Union about another arms agreement (SALT II) to build on the one Nixon signed in 1972, the Soviets, blatantly ignoring Carter's simultaneous appeal for the Soviets to improve their record on human rights, initiated a crackdown against dissidents such as Sakharov and Anatoly Sharansky. Genuinely upset by the crackdown—and aware that domestic political support for détente was severely harmed by the Soviet actions—Carter called the trials and imprisonments an attack "on every human being in the world who believes in basic human freedoms."[11]

On June 7, while working on the Middle East negotiations, the president delivered a speech in Annapolis in which he pointedly referred to the costs of the Soviets' "disruptive behavior" in the world. After criticizing their violation of human rights, Carter painted a dire picture of Soviet expansionism in Africa: "The Soviet Union apparently sees military power and military assistance as the best means of expanding their influence abroad." Soviet leaders were furious about Carter's rhetoric.[12] The Soviets had heard this kind of talk from Carter before, but never seemed to be as bothered as they were now. This time Carter's tone seemed to be different. "They finally heard you," National Security Adviser Brzezinski wrote the president.[13]

. . .

There were some occasions when any Democrat would have had trouble given the changing political balance of the era. Labor legislation to strengthen the National Labor Relations Board that Carter had proposed the previous summer and that the House had passed quickly had stalled in the Senate. The AFL-CIO conducted a massive lobbying operation to get the bill passed. President Carter, who had an uneasy relationship with labor, believing that unions exhibited some of the same problems as other organized forces in American politics, put aside his qualms and threw his weight behind the bill. He lobbied senators personally and made this a priority for his administration.

Yet organized labor was not as strong as it had been just one decade earlier. Union membership was rapidly declining as the manufacturing sector of the economy struggled. At the same time, the business community had undertaken a huge effort in the early 1970s to organize interest group representation. When business opponents and their Senate supporters stepped up their efforts to block the bill, labor found itself outmuscled, and Carter was unable to reverse this. The legislation was defeated by what Carter called, "The most expensive and powerful lobby ever mounted against a bill in the nation's history."[14]

National health insurance was another uphill battle in an era of changing political loyalties, rampant inflation, and growing conservative strength. It also turned out to be the issue, more than any other, that created huge fissures between Carter and congressional liberals. There were two competing proposals on health care circulating in the Democratic Party and immense pressure to pass a national health insurance bill. One option, promoted by Senator Kennedy and organized labor, sought to provide federal health insurance for all Americans, financed by federal taxes, while the second would impose a government mandate on all employers to provide coverage for workers, along with a plan to cover catastrophic illness. Both proposals would implement cost controls.

In his first year, Carter had postponed action on health care, saying that stabilizing the economy and taming inflation had to come first. He also rejected Kennedy's proposal, which would depend on federal funds. Mindful as always of the costs of any government program, Carter felt that an outlay of the size needed for comprehensive national health insurance would be not only fiscally irresponsible but also a political impossibility. Carter and Kennedy met several times in the spring and summer of 1978 trying to reach some kind of agreement. The two men had a tense phone conversation on June 26. The senator warned against the kind of incremental reforms that Carter was favoring. Kennedy recalled saying, "I don't think you can go to an elderly group and say, 'You're in . . . the second phase [of coverage], but if we pass the first [phase] and if hospitals keep their costs down and the economy doesn't go so much into a deficit, then you might be phased in.'" Kennedy, who felt that Carter "loved to give the *appearance* of listening," became extraordinarily frustrated.[15] The last meeting took place in July, when Carter rejected a compromise proposed by Kennedy. The senator, furious with the president, said that Carter had displayed a "failure of leadership" on the issue, and the two sides suffered an open internal war.[16]

Relations between the president and most congressional Democrats continued to disintegrate. By the summer of 1978, Ann Dye
from the legislative liaison office was telling her boss, Frank Moore,
that Carter did not have any "natural constituency" in Congress
and that many legislators "personally resent the *anti-Washington
thrust of the 1976 campaign.*" Some of the problems she was hearing
about included fears of "angry taxpayers" and the perception that
the president was "weak, not in control, and indecisive." She noted
that in Congress "if a *perceived* problem is verbalized long enough,
it *becomes* a problem."[17]

That summer, the president invited Gerald Rafshoon to return
to the White House in order to help him revitalize the political
standing of the administration. Rafshoon, who said that he returned
to "save the President's ass," worked to rebuild Carter's media
image. In addition, Carter revamped Frank Moore's legislative
liaison staff.[18]

• • •

During the summer and fall, trouble was also brewing in Iran.
The tense history of U.S.-Iranian relations dated back to 1953. The
CIA had played a pivotal role in a coup against the democratically
elected government of Mohammad Mossadegh, which had developed ties to the Soviet Union. The United States sought to install
a regime that would be sympathetic to Western interests and
helped put into place the Shah Mohammad Reza Pahlavi. The
shah's strong ties to the United States were solidified in the early
1970s, when Richard Nixon and Gerald Ford relied on allies such
as Iran to create a balance of power in the Persian Gulf region and
Iranian oil was a much desired commodity. The shah, in turn, had
come to depend on U.S. weapons like the F-16 and F-18 fighter
planes. Many Iranians, however, despised the shah's efforts to
modernize the country in the 1960s, as well as his willingness to
silence critics through the secret police (SAVAK) that harassed,
abused, and injured citizens.

The Ayatollah Ruhollah Khomeini, an Islamic cleric, emerged

as the leader of the anti-shah forces. During the 1970s, when the ayatollah was in exile in Iraq, his supporters had smuggled cassette tapes of his speeches into Iran to spread his message. By September, middle-class Iranians, university students, and Islamic revolutionaries were in full revolt. U.S. commentators had missed the fact that millions of Iranians had become followers of the Islamic religion—and of the ayatollah.[19] While some American policy makers saw the revolution as part of an explosion of Muslim influence in the region, most members of the Carter administration evaluated the crisis through the lens of the Cold War. Some believed that Khomeini had been directly supported by the Soviet Union; others feared that any instability opened opportunities for the Soviets to influence governments in the region.[20]

Zbigniew Brzezinski, observing these events from Washington, warned of the "arc of crisis" that threatened the Persian Gulf—with the arc extending from Afghanistan all the way to the Horn of Africa. Ever since the British pulled out of the Middle East in the late 1960s, the United States had become extremely concerned about this critical oil-rich region, relying on Iran and Israel to serve as pillars of support in the area. If the Iranian pillar collapsed, or so the White House's Cold War logic went, the Soviets would be able to gain a more solid foothold in the region and threaten the energy-dependent United States.

• • •

The administration hoped that a breakthrough in the Middle East could become its most lasting accomplishment. Carter brought the Israeli and Egyptian leadership together at Camp David from September 5 to September 17. The meeting was not scripted and was largely unplanned. By this time, Carter was willing to work with Begin rather than around him. The stakes were high; a peace agreement could have a big political payoff. Carter was prepared to find out what Begin was willing to accept.[21]

Embracing the secrecy that they once decried in their campaign against Gerald Ford and Henry Kissinger, the administration advisers decided to meet at Camp David, an extremely secluded spot with only limited media access. State Department spokesman Hodding Carter III, who was the son of a liberal southern journalist, had been active in the civil rights movement during the 1960s, and had worked on Carter's presidential campaign, wanted to avoid debilitating leaks and thus ensure diplomatic success.[22] The negotiations were intense. Carter acted as go-between, often finding himself defending each of the leaders to the other and trying to explain how differing political systems resulted in different pressures.[23]

Though they initially deliberated as a group, Carter started to meet with each leader separately when it appeared that this was the most productive strategy. Carter's relationship with Sadat was much better than his relationship with Begin. Carter saw Sadat as a heroic figure willing to take an enormous risk, and the two men developed a natural affinity. Carter did become more comfortable with Begin over time, but he never really liked him. As with Rabin, Carter simply saw Begin as less daring than Sadat.

Carter began the Camp David meetings by insisting on a comprehensive peace plan that included territorial disputes between the Egyptians and Israelis as well as the conflicts between Israel and the Palestinians over the West Bank. Without addressing the latter issue, Carter did not think that the three parties would be able to achieve peace in the region given that, in his mind, the anger over the Israeli relationship with the Palestinians was the heart of Arab anger toward the Jewish state. Carter, however, soon realized that focusing on the Sinai Peninsula offered the best, if not the only, opportunity to reach a viable deal. He dropped the Israeli-Palestinian issue. Toward the end of the meetings, Sadat was ready to leave in frustration because there had been no progress on the issue of Israeli settlements in the West Bank, a problem that he also thought was essential to establishing peace and one that he needed to demonstrate his concern about if he wanted to retain his credibility within the Arab populace.

In a last-minute act to save the discussions, Carter implored

Sadat to stay, and he obtained an agreement from the Israelis that they would put the issue of settlements before the Knesset for a vote. Carter warned Sadat that leaving would end the relationship between the United States and Egypt. He went so far as to say that it would end their personal friendship.[24] The thirteen-day negotiations produced a "Framework for Peace in the Middle East." The agreement outlined basic goals, including an Israeli withdrawal from the Sinai and an Egyptian recognition of Israel. The agreement left out the crucial issue of the future of the West Bank and Gaza.

The Camp David negotiations boosted Carter's ratings, but not for long. When Hamilton Jordan publicly boasted in May that the administration had "broken the back of the Israeli Lobby," he triggered an angry response from American Jews. According to one Florida attorney, "the Jewish (or Israeli) lobby will remain viable and vigorous, back unbroken, in Congress and the Executive branch long after January 20, 1981, which, in any event, will see your departure from the White House, if indeed, you have not left sooner than that."[25]

After the Camp David meetings, the negotiations over the peace agreement ground to a halt. Although the Israeli Knesset had approved the framework for peace, Israeli prime minister Menachem Begin authorized the construction of more settlements near the West Bank—a direct violation of the spirit of the discussions. Meanwhile, Egyptian president Anwar Sadat started to rethink his willingness at the Camp David discussions to separate the Palestinian issue from the other questions being discussed. He feared that Egypt and his regime would become isolated from the Arab world. By late October, the talks had broken down.

· · ·

Accomplishments like the Panama Canal treaties or the Camp David Accords were soon overshadowed by domestic problems and growing tensions between congressional Democrats and the

White House. Carter was not holding his party together. In October, the president angered many Democrats with how he handled the public works legislation that Congress had considered in his first year. The original proposal called for mandating a specific unemployment level and requiring the government to achieve those numbers through public works spending. Many administration economists, such as Charles Schultze, opposed the measure on the grounds that, like a higher minimum wage, it would aggravate inflation. Others in the administration agreed that combating inflation must be the priority. According to Gerald Rafshoon, "It is impossible to overestimate the importance of the inflation issue to your presidency. It affects every American in a very palpable way. It causes insecurity and anxiety. It affects the American Dream."[26]

Carter agreed to a watered-down version of the bill, which authorized modest levels of public works spending but also made a commitment to achieving a balanced budget. The new version of the bill offered soft long-term targets for unemployment rather than mandates, and constrained unemployment policies by linking them to the current rate of inflation.[27] On October 24, the president made a televised speech in which he called for spending cuts, wage and price guidelines, and other measures aimed at controlling inflation. Once again, jobs would have to take a backseat to economic stabilization.

The compromise on the public works bill left few satisfied. It also reflected a larger and growing division among Democrats. Since FDR, Democrats had always tried to balance the demands of balanced budgets and government spending. Facing rampant inflation in the 1970s, however, and sharing in the distrust of government that spread in the wake of Vietnam and Watergate, Carter tilted the balance toward budgetary restraint. As a "new" Democrat, Carter believed in the need for fiscal conservatism. He found himself at odds with congressional Democrats who still believed that the primary responsibility of the government— especially in hard economic times—was to alleviate the social and

economic inequities facing the nation, even if that meant temporary deficits.

Just as his belief in the primacy of fiscal conservatism put
Carter at odds with many congressional Democrats, so too did his
interest in government reform. Reform was an issue that offered
minimal political payoffs to elected officials as concerns about
the economy replaced concerns about corruption. Carter, nonetheless, pressed forward with the Ethics in Government Act in 1978, a
response to Watergate that established ethics guidelines for executive branch officials and created the Office of the Independent
Counsel to independently investigate corruption. Congressional
Democrats, many of whom were being investigated in 1978 for a
scandal involving a South Korean lobbyist named Tongsun Park,
were more than happy to move on from the legislation once it
passed.

In some cases the president entered into unexpected alliances
with liberals who were also willing to break with core domestic
policies that Democrats had supported for decades. This was the
case with deregulation, a policy that had the support of liberals
such as Senator Kennedy and consumer activist Ralph Nader,
both of whom believed governmental bodies had been captured
by the industries they were supposed to tame. The Airline Deregulation Act, which Congress passed in October, transformed the
industry by allowing for competitive fare setting, phasing out the
Civil Aeronautics Board, and allowing new companies to enter
the marketplace. But in most cases, the president found himself at
odds with the liberal base of the party.

. . .

On the eve of the midterm elections of 1978, Carter admitted
that he had made some mistakes in his first two years. He felt that
he had been overly optimistic about presidential powers and not
sensitive enough to the influence of Congress.[28] The condition of
the economy was the greatest albatross on the White House.
Although the year had started with some evidence that economic

conditions were stabilizing, stock prices declined the last two weeks of August by over one hundred points and the Federal Reserve, defying the president, raised interest rates on November 1. One poll reported that a mere 26 percent of the nation supported his economic policies.[29]

The midterm results were not good for the administration. Democrats retained control of both chambers (59–41 in the Senate and 277–158 in the House), but beneath the surface there was trouble. Republicans increased their numbers in the House (by fifteen seats) and Senate (by three seats). Conservative Republicans from the South and Southwest—who were winning support from former Democrats—were the most notable victors. Conservatives were victorious in Colorado, Iowa, Minnesota, and New Hampshire.[30]

Conservative organizations had played an important role in several races. The National Conservative Political Action Committee (founded in 1975) bankrolled several successful conservative candidates, including Senator Gordon Humphrey of New Hampshire. Thirteen of the twenty senators who were up for reelection and had supported the Panama Canal treaties lost or decided not to run. One of the leading human rights legislators, Minnesota's Donald Fraser, lost. Conservative veterans in the GOP, by contrast, did well,[31] and new Republican legislators, such as Representative Newt Gingrich of Georgia, swept into office with a determination to recapture control of government.

. . .

One week after the elections, Carter finally signed his energy legislation into law, almost a year after he had proposed it. After the House and Senate conference committee had finished with the measures, the legislation was not in the condition that he had hoped for. When Congress passed the watered-down legislation, all that remained were relatively noncontroversial provisions such as deregulating natural gas and tax incentives to encourage new energy sources. Key parts of the original proposal, such as the use of taxation to force conservation, were gone. The political cost of the legislation was immense. Liberal Democrats were unhappy that pricing had been deregulated. Environmental organizations were not pleased because of their opposition to promoting the development of coal and nuclear power. The press criticized Carter for poor legislative skills.[32]

The euphoria that surrounded Carter's walk along Pennsylvania Avenue on Inauguration Day had disappeared by December. The final month of the congressional term was brutal. Carter aggravated tensions with both Soviets and conservatives when he announced the normalization of relations with China. Carter was excited about the move. Brzezinski proclaimed it "a historic chance to start shaping a new global system, with the United States as its predominant coordinator if no longer the paramount power."[33] But the optimism seemed badly misplaced. Many Americans didn't agree with the outreach to China and were furious with the state of foreign policy. Half of the nation believed that the Soviets were stronger than the United States, with 53 percent feeling that the United States needed more aggressive policies toward the Soviets.[34]

During the Democratic midterm convention in Memphis in December, delegates had practically revolted against the president. Senator Ted Kennedy, contemplating a run for the presidency in 1980, took advantage of the mood of the times. He delivered a barnstorming speech in which he lambasted the budget cuts being pushed by Carter to fight inflation and offered a firm defense of social programs. Castigating the administration, Kennedy said that the Democratic Party needed to "sail against the wind" of conservative public sentiment by using the federal government to help alleviate social problems. Carter, in contrast, told the delegates, "It is an illusion to believe we can preserve a commitment to compassionate, progressive government if we fail to bring inflation under control."

Just one month after Congress had passed Carter's energy bill, OPEC officials said that they would raise oil prices again. The regime of the shah of Iran, a U.S. ally since the 1950s, was collapsing in November under the force of an Islamic revolution. Secretary of State Vance reported to Carter on December 2 that American property was being attacked in Iran. General Robert "Dutch" Huyser, who had been deputy commander in chief in the U.S. European Command in the 1970s and who had worked closely with the shah, met with Iranian military officials and recommended that the president start talking with Khomeini given how bad the situation had become.

During a press conference on December 7, Carter made an off-hand remark that caught the attention of Iranians. When a reporter asked him if he thought the shah would survive, Carter responded, "We personally prefer that the Shah maintain a major role in the government but that's a decision for the Iranian people to make." Carter followed the advice of Brzezinski and National Security Council (NSC) staffer Gary Sick, both of whom argued that the proper course of action was to support the shah and encourage him to crack down on the militants.[35] On December 28, Brzezinski told Carter that the "disintegration of Iran would be the most massive American defeat since the beginning of the Cold War, overshadowing in its real consequences the setback in Vietnam."[36]

By the end of his second year, Carter was facing a rebellion from his own party and real pressure from his conservative opponents, who were now looking like a serious force. It was a politically dangerous combination. The economic context of his presidency—an ongoing energy crisis and stagflation—created a public mood that was increasingly disenchanted with the White House. Unfortunately for Carter, the worst was yet to come.

6

Falling Apart

This crisis is a crisis in every sense. It is a crisis for
your Presidency, for the hostages, and for our
country's image around the world.

—Hamilton Jordan (1979)

The mood of the country was not good in January 1979. The
economy remained in terrible shape, with inflation still on the rise,
and there was little sense that things would get better. The Soviet
empire seemed to be expanding, while U.S. influence diminished
as the nation was haunted by the memories of Vietnam. Carter,
according to *Time* magazine, "is markedly older in appearance now,
his wispy, blown-dry hair a shade grayer than it was a year ago. The
sagging skin around his neck adds years to his appearance and is
accentuated by a recent loss of weight, the result of his 30 miles of
weekly jogging to ward off the fatigue of his job. Much of the fresh-
ness is gone, washed away by criticism, defeats, frustration and the
cacophony of demands aimed at him."[1]

Carter's decision to make inflation his top priority pushed most
other domestic initiatives to the side. In October, before the midterm elections, Carter had already taken a number of steps in this

direction, including his appointment of an inflation czar, the economist Alfred Kahn, and a speech in which he assured the country that he would cut the size of the deficit to $33 billion by fiscal year 1980.[2]

Domestic policy adviser Stuart Eizenstat and others in the White House had been shocked and disappointed when they learned in December that the deficit would be 50 percent higher than they had anticipated.[3] On January 4, Eizenstat told the Woman's National Democratic Club, "Our party, and the President who carries the party's banner proudly, face a new era—an era in which we will continue to build on the traditional beliefs and commitments of our party and continue to extend hope to those in need, but in which we must adjust, as difficult as that may be, to new realities."[4]

In his State of the Union address, Carter proclaimed that "we must stop excessive government growth, and we must control government spending habits."[5] Core Democratic constituencies such as organized labor, Catholic working-class voters, and African Americans, already struggling with high unemployment and high inflation, were not pleased. They felt that unemployment remained the most pressing problem and that by cutting spending the government would hurt those suffering worst from the economic downturn. Louis Martin, the president's special liaison to the African American community, reported to Carter that "many national and local leaders, including some Black elected officials, are placing most of the blame for the current unrest on the widely publicized 'austere' budget. . . . They do not buy the linkage between the battle on inflation and the need to cut job programs."[6] Carter delivered the speech, as one reporter noted, still unable "to lay claim to the unshakable support of any single constituency. Even though the legislative branch is filled with members of his own party, they received his speech with almost as little enthusiasm as they showed the pariah Richard Nixon in his last State of the Union message in 1974."[7] Making matters even trickier politically, notwithstanding Carter's new fiscally hawkish posture, the administration remained hesitant about taking all the steps that were needed to seriously curb prices, such as federal pay caps on the milk and sugar industries.[8]

Meanwhile, Carter's attention was split between trying to resolve the domestic economic crisis and looking for an overseas breakthrough that could define his legacy. It didn't look like Iran would be the place. The shah of Iran departed for Egypt on January 16, as the forces supporting Khomeini seized control. The revolutionaries celebrated by flooding the streets and publicly declaring their loyalty to the ayatollah. On February 1, the ayatollah returned to Iran from exile and was greeted by millions of supporters who lined the streets. By the middle of the month, Khomeini controlled the military.

The Middle East seemed to be a better bet. After Camp David, President Sadat and Prime Minister Begin both understood that they were facing a unique opportunity to achieve a historic agreement. Failure would strengthen opponents of peace in the region who would claim that treaties with Israel would never work. Vice President Mondale continued urging the president to abandon the project, warning that there would be no good outcome diplomatically or politically. But, according to Brzezinski, Carter did not want to back down. In certain respects, Mondale's warnings only motivated him to try harder.[9]

A new round of discussions occurred on March 1 and 2 in Washington. When Begin arrived at Andrews Air Force Base, he explained that Israel would not be pressured into signing a "sham document." The night that Begin arrived, Carter told a group of governors that the Middle East negotiation was "one of the most frustrating and discouraging experiences I have ever had in my life. . . . It is just disgusting almost to feel that we are that close and can't quite get it."[10] Their first meeting was so bad that they canceled a second meeting that was scheduled for later that day. But the mood improved the next morning. Begin conceded on several points. For instance, he agreed to a twelve-month "goal" for a deal with the Palestinians.[11]

Building on the momentum, a few weeks after the meetings at

Andrews Air Force Base, the president traveled to the Middle East. His trip to Cairo was especially successful. By contrast, in Jerusalem he was greeted by protesters who carried signs that read "Carter Go Home."[12] Once again, the subsequent meeting with Begin was not cordial. When the two men met in Begin's private study, the prime minister again warned that he was not prepared to sign any treaty until the Knesset had an opportunity to debate the issues. "I couldn't believe it," Carter wrote in his diary on March 10. "I stood up and asked him if it was necessary for me to stay any longer. We then spent about 45 minutes on our feet in his study. I asked him if he actually wanted a peace treaty, because my impression was that everything he could do to obstruct it, he did with apparent relish."[13] Carter felt that with the next presidential election approaching he was on an extremely tight political timeline. He was pushing aside other issues to focus on this. Begin did not appear to feel rushed.

In the end, Carter achieved a breakthrough.[14] The agreement he brokered stipulated that Israel would remove its troops from the Sinai and that Egypt would recognize Israel and open diplomatic channels. The president won Begin's support by leaving the issue of Jewish settlements and the status of the West Bank outside of the agreement and promising Israel, as well as Egypt, substantial financial and military assistance. Israel was also guaranteed that the United States would supply them with oil should the Egyptians cut off supply lines that they controlled.

The historic handshake between Anwar Sadat and Menachem Begin in front of the White House on March 26 generated excitement around the world. All three television networks covered the event live. In Jerusalem and Tel Aviv, Israelis flooded the streets to dance to folk music and sing nationalistic songs, but most Arab countries opposed the treaties. Damascus radio called it a "traitor's treaty." A few hours before Begin departed, a civilian was killed in Jerusalem by a bomb. Fourteen others were injured. In the United States, many conservatives and liberal Jewish Democrats feared that the agreement signaled diminished support for Israel but, given public enthusiasm for the accord, they remained quiet. Edward

Sanders, Carter's liaison with Jewish organizations, reported that the community "recognizes the historic significance of the peace treaty and is appreciative of your personal contribution. However, support for the Administration is *tentative* and *wary*."[15]

• • •

The euphoria over the accord faded quickly. By April, when Carter put forth another energy program, the general mood of the country was sour. Approximately 50 percent of the gas stations in the United States did not have fuel and the stations that had fuel were charging prices that were 50 percent more than the year before. Drivers were forced to line up for gas, frequently for over an hour, on specified days.

President Carter's new energy plan included decontrolling prices and a windfall profits tax on oil companies to finance mass transportation and subsidize fuel for lower-income families. Carter also proposed the development of alternative energy sources and new mechanisms for energy conservation. The plan revolved around the theme of sacrifice: consumers would be forced to accept higher prices and use less energy.

While there was initial support for the plan, opponents quickly mobilized. New England Democrats opposed to higher heating prices in what was a very bitter winter allied with southern Democrats who rejected the windfall profits tax. Many Republicans joined in this coalition. With gas shortages spreading throughout the country, Carter's proposal for more sacrifice did not sit well with his party.[16]

Carter also confronted protests when one of his options for energy independence—nuclear power—came under intense scrutiny after a nuclear meltdown at Pennsylvania's Three Mile Island reactor on March 28. People living in the area were told to either evacuate or stay sealed up indoors. Within a month of the accident, environmental activists were marching throughout the country demanding that nuclear facilities be shut down. On April 29, about 280 protesters, including former Pentagon official Daniel Ellsberg, were arrested at a Colorado nuclear weapons plant. "A major nuclear plant accident would kill 45,000 persons immediately and tens of thousands of deaths would follow as cancer and leukemia took their toll over 30 years," warned the famous pediatrician and author Benjamin Spock, who headed a similar protest in Arkansas.[17]

As the times got tough, critics started to come out of the woodwork. One of Carter's former top speechwriters, James Fallows, published a widely publicized article entitled "The Passionless Presidency" for the cover story of the *Atlantic* in May 1979. Picking up on themes that had haunted Carter since his gubernatorial years, Fallows depicted his former boss as a politician who lacked positions, often couldn't see the forest for the trees, and who was not particularly talented in dealing with Congress or the art of governing. According to the article, the president had also become so focused on international policy that he was bored with key domestic issues like inflation. The article caused a big stir, fueling conversations about these charges.

Despite his efforts to fulfill campaign promises to women's and African American organizations, Carter had trouble maintaining the support of either constituency. Since becoming president, he had appointed an unprecedented number of women to senior positions in the executive branch and he had lobbied to build support for the ratification of the Equal Rights Amendment. Yet Carter's failure to take a stand against 1976 legislation that prohibited the use of federal funds for abortions and his reticence to support domestic violence legislation caused immense frustration among feminists. His efforts to position himself in the center won him only enemies, not friends.

There were similar problems with African Americans. Carter did demonstrate his support for civil rights in a number of ways. His government reorganization plan centralized the enforcement of civil rights policies. Carter also supported the creation of a minority contract set-aside program in 1977, which stipulated that 10 percent of public works appropriations had to be given to minority-owned enterprises. Yet in other instances, Carter always seemed to do wrong. The president opposed school busing and refused to offer substantive support to urban policy or full employment. The Congressional Black Caucus was unhappy after leaks from the White House indicated that Carter's advisers had hesitated before reaching his decision to support affirmative action when a challenge reached the Supreme Court in 1978. With both liberal women's and civil rights groups, Carter's shift away from unemployment and toward deficit reduction dampened their enthusiasm for the White House.[18]

Senator Ted Kennedy was openly critical of the administration. The previous year's health care battle had proved the final straw for Kennedy. The senator planned a challenge to the president in the primaries just as Reagan had taken on Ford. In June, Carter told a group of congressmen that if Kennedy ran against him, he would "whip his ass." But other members of the administration were not so confident.

The energy crisis was weighing down heavily on the administration. While polls showed that most Americans did not believe there was a crisis, the daily life of anyone using fuel was miserable. Some Californians, one of the states worst hit by the crisis, camped out overnight to get gas, and a pregnant woman was physically assaulted after someone believed she had cut in line. The rest of the economy was in terrible shape as well with inflation reaching almost 13 percent and most industries, including automobiles, suffering from plummeting sales.[19]

The president's political struggles were also not abating. When Carter began his effort to finalize a second Strategic Arms Limitations Talk (SALT II) treaty, he had already spent most of his political capital on securing the Panama Canal treaties, and Senate moderates were unwilling to engage in another pitched fight on his behalf. Senator Henry Jackson sent a memo, drafted by his staffer Richard Perle, outlining specific demands that should be made of the Soviets if Carter wanted the Senate's support. The memo, which circulated throughout the administration, constituted a strong warning about how much opposition on SALT II

Carter would face.[20] Although proponents of SALT II organized a private lobby called Americans for SALT, they were outdone by the Committee on the Present Danger, a well-financed and skilled group of neoconservative policy makers that claimed the support of about 175 legislators.[21]

Carter's decision to normalize relations with China, intended to pressure the Soviets into an agreement, instead had the effect of heightening tensions. It was one of the main issues of discussion when Soviet premier Leonid Brezhnev and Carter met in Vienna in June. Brezhnev told Carter that Soviet-American relations would "suffer" if Chinese-American relations were not handled carefully.[22] Nonetheless, the Soviet leader, ailing and old beyond his years, wanted to strike a deal. He told Carter, "If we do not succeed, God will not forgive us."

Carter and Brezhnev reached an agreement on June 18. They completed work on several issues that had been excluded from the 1972 SALT treaty by establishing numerical equality in delivery systems for nuclear weapons and creating limitations on certain missiles. Republicans and neoconservative Democrats were unhappy when they saw the photograph of the two leaders and heard the details of the agreement. The Senate Foreign Relations Committee passed the treaty by a narrow margin of 9–6, but only after holding contentious hearings and adding various stipulations and provisions to limit its impact. The Senate Armed Services Committee produced a critical analysis that warned the treaty would work against American "national security interests."[23]

• • •

To try to build support for his energy program, which he still believed to be one of his most important initiatives, Carter wrote a speech outlining his plan and explaining that the energy crisis was part of a larger moral dilemma facing the nation. By this time, the president was in deep trouble at home. His approval rating stood at 33 percent. Patrick Caddell, convinced there was a psychic crisis afflicting the soul of Americans after Vietnam, Watergate, and inflation, had been lobbying the president since the spring to make such a speech. Caddell had been influenced by many books, including the historian Christopher Lasch's best seller *The Culture of Narcissism*. The book traced the decline of the work ethic and the rise of a narcissistic culture. Although Caddell misread the book, believing it was about selfishness as opposed to Lasch's more esoteric concern about the vanishing sense of self, Lasch's overall points about the culture's current crisis of confidence had a big impact. Caddell had also been influenced by the writing of the political scientist James MacGregor Burns, who argued that a "transformational" leader "seeks to satisfy higher needs, and engages the full person of the follower." "This crisis," Caddell said, is "in many ways dwarfed by what Lincoln and Roosevelt faced, yet in many ways the reverse is true, for there are no armies to be dispatched or millions to be given jobs."[24]

The speech writing did not go smoothly. During one dinner party with a group of academic and media experts, which included the sociologist Daniel Bell, Christopher Lasch, Bill Moyers, Haynes Johnson (*Washington Post*), John Gardner (Common Cause), Charles Peters (*Washington Monthly*), and Jesse Jackson, the group could not come up with an effective message on the energy and economic crisis.[25] "Nobody wants to hear it," said Rosalynn upon reading the first draft; "they've heard about new energy programs ever since you've been in office, and prices are still going up. They don't want to hear about a new program that will allocate energy to the elderly at a lower cost. They just want to be told that everything is going to be all right and that somebody understands the situation and has it under control."[26]

Carter listened to her advice. Only thirty hours before his speech was scheduled on July 5, the White House informed the television networks that it was postponed. The president retreated to Camp David, where he invited a wide range of experts and politicians to advise him about what he was doing wrong. Arkansas governor Bill Clinton told Carter that voters in his state had less of a sense of who he was in 1979 than in 1976.[27] Vice President

Mondale did not think that the meetings or the speech was a good idea. Washington insider Clark Clifford, watching as the president sat on the floor and scribbled down notes as people spoke to him, couldn't help but think that it would have been inconceivable to imagine "Lyndon Johnson sitting on the floor and saying, 'Tell me what I am doing wrong.' "[28] Speechwriter Hendrik Hertzberg had himself said that "the country does not want or need another energy speech. It wants and needs energy actions."[29]

On July 15, Carter finally made the speech. Over 60 million people tuned in. He offered a series of proposals, such as the creation of an energy security corporation, which would be responsible for developing new kinds of energy sources, and a windfall profits tax to help pay for the energy security measures. An energy mobilization board, to the chagrin of environmentalists who once had high hopes for Carter, would have the power to fast-track the creation of new power plants. But more importantly, Carter told Americans that they faced a crisis of confidence and urged them to recognize—and to accept—that their families lived in an age of limits:

> The threat is nearly invisible in ordinary ways. It is a crisis of confidence. It is a crisis that strikes at the very heart and soul and spirit of our national will. We can see this crisis in the growing doubt about the meaning of our own lives and in the loss of a unity of purpose for our nation. The erosion of our confidence in the future is threatening to destroy the social and the political fabric of America.

The speech drew mixed responses. Some reporters thought that Carter had one of his finest moments. Others felt that Carter, in his monotone delivery, blamed the nation for the problems they were struggling with rather than offering solutions and leadership.

Two days after the speech, Carter asked thirty-four top officials to resign. Five accepted, including Michael Blumenthal of Treasury, Joseph Califano of HEW, James Schlesinger of Energy,

Brock Adams of Transportation, and Attorney General Griffin
Bell. Califano, a former LBJ official, was a favorite of liberals, who
were disappointed with his resignation. Carter named Hamilton
Jordan to serve as his chief of staff.

The media and pundits did not have many good things to say
about the resignations, and they undermined any goodwill about
the July 15 speech, which was now being called "the speech." Carter's request for the mass resignations seemed to indicate that he
had lost control of the White House. The July 15 speech and the
resignations became linked together. The negative coverage fit into
a broader narrative about a failed presidency that colored much of
the reporting on Carter in 1979.[30] The energy proposals that the
president offered in his speech became bogged down in Congress
for more than a year. Eventually, Congress passed the Crude Oil
Windfall Profit Tax Act and the Energy Security Act in 1980.

• • •

In this unhappy environment, small events turned into big political explosions. UN ambassador Andrew Young triggered one such
firestorm when he met with a PLO representative on July 26. The
meeting had not been authorized by the administration. In August,
the president asked Young to resign. African American groups were
livid, and Jewish organizations were even more distrustful of Carter.
They perceived Young's actions as further proof that Carter was
unsympathetic to Israel.

Then there was Cuba. In late July and August, as the Senate
slowly deliberated on SALT II, Democrats Richard Stone and
Frank Church, chair of the Senate Foreign Relations Committee
and presidential aspirant, announced that there were intelligence
reports showing a Soviet brigade of about two thousand men
stationed in Cuba.

Both men saw that there was political value in taking a tough
stance against the Cubans and Soviets. Church, who wanted to
run for president again in 1980, thought that he could use the
Soviet brigade to position himself as tough on foreign policy and

to appeal to the conservative electorate of his home state, Idaho. Richard Stone, a Florida Democrat with a vulnerable seat and an estimated five hundred thousand anti-Castro Cuban émigrés in his state, had been hawkish on Cuba since entering the Senate.

Most experts agreed that the brigade did not threaten national security. The forces had been in Cuba since 1962 and were permitted under the agreement that followed the Cuban Missile Crisis. Clark Clifford concluded, "This entire business about the Soviet brigade in Cuba is a false issue."[31] On September 7, Carter told reporters that the United States had a right to ask that the brigade be removed. Yet, he said, "It is not an assault force, it does not have airlift or sea-going capabilities and does not have weapons capable of attacking the United States." This kind of analytic response did not work. Even a group of senior security experts agreed that although senators should never have claimed that the brigade constituted a crisis, the release of the information to the public placed SALT in jeopardy.[32] Carter's opponents said that the brigade was further proof the Soviets could not be trusted and that signing SALT II posed a serious risk to the nation. Carter's hard work on détente seemed further endangered.

· · ·

In the early fall, the president confronted another dilemma when he came under intense pressure to allow the shah of Iran to enter the United States. Carter had thus far resisted any such appeals, fearing that taking this action would trigger an enormous backlash against America. When Carter learned, however, that the shah was suffering from lymphoma and requesting medical treatment in New York City, his stance changed slightly. Henry Kissinger and David Rockefeller, both of whom had worked with the shah in the 1970s and who had wanted him in the United States before the illness, lobbied the president to admit him for treatment. On October 23, the shah arrived in New York. Two days later, he had surgery.

Upon learning that the shah had entered the country, supporters of the ayatollah feared a repeat of the 1953 coup. Photos circulated in Iran of a healthy-looking shah, suggesting the admission into the United States for medical treatment was a cover-up to rescue the fallen leader and somehow plot for his return.[33]

On November 4, Iranian students stormed the American embassy in Tehran. They captured over fifty soldiers and diplomats. A hostage crisis had begun. Upon telling the president the situation, Hamilton Jordan—who was struggling against accusations that he had used cocaine at a New York nightclub—predicted that this would be a defining issue for the administration and in the 1980 election.[34]

Secretary Vance, fearing that domestic electoral considerations would push the president toward a hawkish stand, urged the president to avoid using force. While driving home from the White House along Massachusetts Avenue on the third day of the crisis, Jordan's driver rode past the Iranian embassy. As Jordan slouched in the back of the car so that he was not seen, he watched hundreds of Americans chanting, "Let our people go!" Jordan recalled that he "felt the anger of that crowd and I saw it etched on every face. Their rage, their very presence seemed to be saying, 'We've had enough.'"[35] The protest suggested to him that Carter had only a limited amount of time before this anger turned toward the administration rather than the Iranians.

One bright spot, politically, during these difficult days was that Ted Kennedy, Carter's main challenger in the upcoming presidential primaries, appeared to be losing his footing. In a CBS News one-hour special, broadcast the same day that the hostage crisis started, Kennedy did not have a clear answer when reporter Roger Mudd asked him why he wanted to be president. Kennedy later recalled in his memoirs that he had been under the impression this would be a "softball" interview that focused on his family's connection to Cape Cod. As a result, he didn't have any staff present and didn't really prepare. In the first of two interviews, the senator was unable to offer compelling answers to tough questions about the 1969 Chappaquiddick scandal, when he drove off a bridge and the woman traveling with him drowned; Kennedy had left the scene, allegedly discombobulated and seeking assistance. When Mudd asked about the presidency in the second meeting, according to Kennedy, he had "not yet publicly declared my intention to challenge President Carter and had no intention of announcing my candidacy in this interview with Roger Mudd."[36]

But Kennedy's stumbles did not bring much comfort to Carter or his advisers. On the fifth day of the Iranian hostage crisis, Jordan urged the president to cancel a visit to Canada on the grounds that he should focus all of his attention on the Iranian hostages. Carter agreed to do so. Jordan noted that CBS News devoted 55 percent of its coverage the previous night to Iran.[37] The president canceled other appearances as well, including campaign visits to Iowa and New Hampshire. This was a turning point. The president would now be defined by the crisis and by his ability to achieve a resolution. In late December, Carter announced that he would not illuminate the lights on the White House Christmas tree until the hostages were freed.[38]

The television networks devoted unprecedented attention to the hostages, interviewing their families and covering every angle of the daily events. ABC had been quick to move, sending a reporter to Tehran immediately. ABC's first nighttime special was viewed by 12 million people. Americans hung yellow ribbons on trees and on their homes to support the hostages.[39]

Initially, the crisis benefited the president. His popularity ratings soared. The reporter Haynes Johnson noted that "Attacks on Carter personally by Iranian leaders, prominently reported via TV to Americans at home, gave the President a stature he had failed to achieve in three years in office. Carter became the personification of the nation, the symbol of American resolve, the rallying point for Americans at home to respond to insults from abroad."[40] Jody Powell and Hodding Carter III played to the media coverage, keeping Carter constantly before the cameras to present the image of a president who was totally focused on bringing the hostages home.[41]

Kennedy further hurt his candidacy when he gave a speech in December criticizing the shah's corrupt government. The speech led many observers to argue that Kennedy lacked patriotism—or, at a minimum, political tact. Adopting the same Rose Garden strategy that Gerald Ford used against Ronald Reagan in the 1976 Republican primaries, Carter continued to cancel appearances in Iowa and New Hampshire.[42] Withdrawing from a debate in Iowa, the president told reporters on *Meet the Press* that in a "time of crisis" he thought "national unity during the Iran crisis would be jeopardized by participation in this partisan event." Jody Powell leaked a memo to a trusted reporter in which he urged the president to participate in the debate. The purpose of the leak was for the reporter to see the handwritten note from Carter that stated, "I can't disagree with any of this but I cannot break away from my duties here which are extraordinary now and ones which only I can fulfill. We will just have to take the adverse political consequences and make the best of it. Right now both Iran and Afghanistan look bad and will need my constant attention." Many reporters criticized the memo as a political ploy, "Nixonian," according to some, in its level of manipulation.[43]

Nonetheless, Carter's advisers believed that he "would win or lose based on how he was seen doing his job in the White House, far more than on what he did on the campaign trail." They realized that how he handled the Iran hostage crisis would have a much bigger role in shaping the electorate than any speeches or appearances he might make on the campaign trail.[44]

Equally important, Carter could afford to stay out of the contest. Besides having the visibility of an incumbent, his organization was superior to Kennedy's, whose offices didn't even have telephones until several days into their campaign.[45] In New Hampshire, Carter relied on the power of the presidency. In contrast to the Carter who vetoed pork barrel spending in his first year as president to the ire of Congress, the administration allocated funds shortly before the primary for highways, ski resorts, and a commuter train.[46]

• • •

On December 27, the Soviets invaded Afghanistan. A coup against Afghan communists the previous year had given Muslim funda-mentalists the reins of government, and the Soviets were seeking to gain control of the rogue nation. Whereas the Soviets were con-cerned about their borders, American policy makers saw the inva-sion as an effort by the Soviets to expand their influence in the region. Carter, who was astounded that the Soviets had launched the invasion, understood that this killed any domestic possibility for détente. Carter told Jordan: "This is more serious, Hamilton. [It] is deliberate aggression that calls into question détente and the way we have been doing business with the Soviets for the past decade."[47]

The invasion also confirmed conservative Republicans' worst warnings about the Soviets. Republican senator Strom Thurmond complained that "the decline in our defense strength as a result of the administration's defense policies and congressional action will make the 1980's a dangerous decade."[48]

The hostage crisis was starting to wear on the president. While advisers had initially hoped for a quick solution, and Carter had enjoyed a boost in approval ratings, the public was also weary of the crisis. The respected CBS Evening News anchor Walter Cronkite began signing off each show in January 1980 by saying how many days the hostages had been captive.

Early in January, Carter asked Senate Majority Leader Robert Byrd to table further discussion of SALT II. During his State of the Union address, Carter outlined the "Carter Doctrine." He called for a 5 percent annual increase in defense spending and outlined a more aggressive posture in the Persian Gulf that would make the region the center of national security policy. Carter also decided that the United States would boycott the Moscow Olympics.

A secret National Security Council document reported that "Moscow has characterized the Administration's posture on Soviet-American relations as the culmination of its long, if erratic, slide toward anti-Sovietism, a slide now accelerated by the upcoming presidential elections." The Soviets, the memo said, had come to stress the "unreliability and inconsistency" of Carter as a negotiating partner.[49] At home, the reaction was different. Carter's approval ratings rose from 32 percent to 61 percent in one month.[50]

• • •

The crisis did not deter Kennedy in his campaign against the president. Kennedy was able to mobilize traditional Democratic constituencies who had been unhappy with the administration's record, while claiming that Carter's inflation-centered domestic programs were little different than what conservatives such as Ronald Reagan proposed. The appointment of Paul Volcker as chairman of the Federal Reserve exacerbated the tensions with liberals because the new chairman was willing to live with unemployment if he could calm prices. On foreign policy, Kennedy attacked the administration for veering from dangerous militarism one day to aimless negotiations on other days. Soon after the president announced the hawkish Carter Doctrine in response to the Soviet invasion, Kennedy delivered a lecture at Georgetown University in which he criticized Carter for speaking aggressively without being prepared to back it up. "Exaggeration and hyperbole," Kennedy warned, "are the enemies of sensible foreign policy."[51]

Carter's goal was to make the primaries look more like a general election. Rather than having Democrats think about sending a message through their caucuses or primaries—as they had done with Carter in 1976—the president wanted them to think about who would be the best president. In Iowa and New Hampshire, Carter's advertisements stressed the Camp David Accords as evidence of his negotiating skills and praised his character, with the goal of implicitly raising questions about Kennedy. "A Solid Man in a Sensitive Job," boasted one ad.[52] Because Carter wasn't spending much time in New Hampshire, he conducted nightly telephone conference calls with voters. "Carter has succeeded with his Iranian thing in actually making it suspect to have a political dialogue," complained a Kennedy worker.[53]

Whatever its costs, the strategy worked. Carter soundly defeated Kennedy in both Iowa on January 21 and New Hampshire on February 26. The next month, Carter won in Florida and Illinois. Kennedy was able to win only in his home state of Massachusetts. As Carter stacked up his victories, his campaign started to stress that only through a "disaster scenario" did Kennedy have a "mathematical" chance of winning.[54]

But Kennedy persisted and found some support. The economy was in terrible shape. Carter's announcement of a new initiative to curb inflation fueled the anger of Kennedy's supporters that the president had a tin ear toward the unemployed, who were likely to be adversely impacted by the new policies.

On March 25, Kennedy won the New York primary and reenergized his campaign. Many Jewish voters had been upset by a controversy that unfolded on March 2, when the UN Security Council had voted on a resolution stating that Israel should dismantle settlements in the occupied territories, including Jerusalem. When the U.S. ambassador voted in favor of the resolution, Jewish organizations were furious. Carter had apologized, though Secretary Vance then defended the decision. Jewish voters had expressed their displeasure by disproportionately supporting Kennedy. Yet the loss was not just about Israel and not just about Jewish voters. The primary reflected a broader problem. Carter seemed to be alienating the core liberal constituency that had put him in the White House at the same time that Ted Kennedy was stepping up his game. As *Washington Post* columnist David Broder wrote, "The longer he [Kennedy] campaigns, the more he sounds like the authentic voice of 1960s liberalism, a passion for what he called 'economic democracy and social justice' that found expression in ambitious, interventionist, activist government programs."[55]

The next important contest took place in Wisconsin on April 1. Observers expected Kennedy to do well given the state's progressive tradition. Hours before voters went to the polls, Carter announced that the administration was finishing a deal to release the hostages. With this news as the backdrop, Carter won. Kennedy's momentum was stifled.

But shortly after the primary, the administration said that the deal had unexpectedly fallen apart. Critics then charged that Carter had politicized the hostage issue. Jody Powell warned Jordan, "Ham—I'm just telling you that we are about to have an enormous credibility problem. The combination of not campaigning and that early-morning announcement had made skeptics out of even our friends in the press."[56] The *New York Times* and the *Washington Post* ran stories investigating the political timing behind Carter's statements. Powell dismissed them as "error, smear and fantasy."[57]

Three weeks after Wisconsin, Kennedy bounced back with narrow victories in Pennsylvania and Michigan. Since Democrats had adopted proportional voting in the 1970s party reforms (rules that granted the loser in each primary a sizable number of delegates), Carter retained his mathematical advantage by building his delegate count. Carter won the next eleven primaries; Kennedy won only the District of Columbia.

But Kennedy refused to quit. Carter could not understand why his arguments about the mathematical impossibility of a Kennedy victory did not persuade his opponent to step out of the race. Charles Kirbo explained that Kennedy would not leave easily: "It takes a lot of guts to stick your neck out and run for any public office, particularly President. But the only thing that's tougher than announcing for office is withdrawing from a race, 'cause when you drop out you are saying that you are quitting and that you're beaten. That's hard for a Kennedy to say."[58] Kennedy declared that Carter had to win one of the major final primaries—California, New Jersey, or Ohio—to prove that he deserved the nomination.[59]

With Carter trying to end the contest with Kennedy, the negotiations over the hostages in Iran broke down in early April. Carter had been working with the new president of Iran, who was seen as more moderate than the ayatollah, while Hamilton Jordan headed negotiations with French and Argentinean intermediaries who maintained close contacts with the Iranian leadership. Khomeini discovered what was going on and killed the discussions. Carter, in response, broke off diplomatic ties and instituted new sanctions on April 7.

Feeling that things were at a complete stalemate, the president finally agreed to listen to Brzezinski's advice and authorize the use of force. While Secretary of State Cyrus Vance was away on a trip to Florida, Carter agreed to a complex mission that involved eight helicopters flying south of Tehran, where they would land and rendezvous with C-130 aircraft that would be carrying supplies for the soldiers and the hostages. A rescue team would drive into Tehran from the landing base, raid the building where the hostages were held, and depart on C-141 airplanes. Carter agreed to the plan on April 11. The mission was top secret. When he learned about the mission upon his return to Washington, Vance told Carter that he would formally resign once the operation was complete, regardless of the outcome. He explained, "I was convinced that the decision was wrong and that it carried great risks for the hostages and our national interests."[60]

Operation Eagle Claw was a disaster. The mission was launched on April 24. Several of the helicopters were stopped by a sandstorm or grounded by mechanical failure halfway into the mission. One of the functioning helicopters crashed into a C-130. Eight men were killed. The mission was a total embarrassment for the United States. The Iranians captured the helicopters that were left behind in the crash and gained control of classified information. Images of the crash played on television, and Carter's critics, on the left and right, said this offered more evidence of his incompetence. The president's approval ratings plummeted below 30 percent.

Carter felt so desperate that he put the Rose Garden strategy on the shelf and went out on the campaign trail. The president defeated Kennedy in Indiana, Tennessee, and North Carolina. The primaries ended on Super Tuesday, June 3. Carter secured 321 delegates, and took West Virginia, Montana, and, most importantly, Ohio, which responded to Kennedy's challenge. Yet Kennedy's victories in California and New Jersey gave his supporters enough confidence to carry on to the convention. Kennedy ignored calls from the president, and when the two men finally met in an effort to reconcile, Carter refused to endorse Kennedy's policy recommendations (such as national health insurance) while Kennedy did not give firm assurances that he would stop campaigning.[61]

As the primaries wound down, Caddell wrote one of his most pessimistic analyses yet. Looking ahead to the general election, he explained that Carter was going to face a Republican Party united around the candidacy of Ronald Reagan. He would also have to contend with a third-party challenge from Republican John Anderson, who had decided to run as an Independent. "The issue structures could not be worse," Caddell wrote. "The public is anxious, confused, hostile, and sour. Pessimism remains high. An unhappy electorate has reflected its overwhelming skepticism by awarding every candidate in 1980 a negative personal rating. . . . More to the point the American people do not want Jimmy Carter as their President. Not forced to choose a specific candidate, voters by almost 2 to 1 would reject Carter as President, a remarkable turn around from 1977, 1978, and much of 1979." Caddell noted that "Carter approaching the 1980 general election appears in profile to be much more the 1976 Gerald Ford than the 1976 Jimmy Carter."[62]

The summer months leading into the convention were some of the worst in Carter's presidency. On July 14, the Justice Department revealed that his brother, Billy, had been required to register as a foreign agent because of his work with Libya, a state known to sponsor terrorism and which was extremely hostile toward Israel. It was reported that Billy Carter had traveled several times to Libya and received hundreds of thousands of dollars from the government and Libyan oil interests. Justice had been investigating the matter for several months. Carter denied knowing about the investigation or about his brother's dealings. The *Washington Post* and *Washington Star* competed on stories, and congressional investigations looked into whether government policy had been affected. Carter had known about one trip in which he said Billy went to try to

obtain the release of hostages. The president was forced to acknowl-
edge that he had known more than he initially admitted. Billy, an
alcoholic, inflamed the situation when he responded with anti-
Semitic comments to a question about whether the scandal would
influence Jewish voters. There was no smoking gun evidence of ille-
gal wrongdoing, but "Billygate" damaged and distracted Carter at a
tense moment in his campaign. "At the time Jimmy should have
been working on his acceptance speech for the approaching Democratic Convention," Rosalynn Carter recalled, "our lawyers had us
both searching through our diaries and files for any mention of Billy
or Libya."[63] Carter finally stopped the bleeding with a skillful performance at a press conference.

As the summer drew to a close, Kennedy supporters made a
last-ditch effort by seeking an "open convention," which allows
delegates to vote for the candidate they choose rather than the
one to whom they had pledged. With unemployment rising, international crises raging, and Billy's troubles multiplying, proponents
of an open convention argued that delegates should have the freedom to change their mind as conditions changed. The push for an
open convention also drew support from followers of Edmund
Muskie and Henry "Scoop" Jackson, each of whom hoped to seize
the advantage if the convention was opened up.

Carter took the struggle for an open convention seriously. His
campaign assembled an extensive whip operation on the convention floor to make sure that delegates did not flip to Kennedy. The
whips repeatedly stressed the connection between the open convention movement and Kennedy's candidacy in order to suggest
that this was little more than a cynical ploy to benefit one politician. They also stressed that altering the rules would take the
party back to the days when conventions were dominated by bosses
rather than voters. On the first day of the convention, delegates
voted against the rule, and the effort to hold an open convention
failed. Carter did, however, have to agree to have Kennedy's progressive economic program on the party platform even though it
starkly contrasted with his own anti-inflation policies. Carter

became the first Democrat to win the nomination since 1896 without the support of New York or Pennsylvania.[64]

In Kennedy's final jab at the nominee, he delivered a rousing speech that called on the party to "renew" its commitment to its founding principles of "economic justice" and reminded his audience that "our cause has been, since the days of Thomas Jefferson, the cause of the common man and the common woman." The crowd gave him a standing ovation. Madison Square Garden was filled with chants of "Ted-dy!"

Carter's speech paled in comparison. It started off on the wrong note when his teleprompter broke. The president could not see the text and his delivery was mechanical and choppy. The nervous president worried that the audience was not with him. When the speech ended, the machine that was supposed to drop balloons down onto the convention floor to celebrate his victory malfunctioned. Nothing came down.

As the convention ended, a large number of Democrats appeared on the stage to stand alongside Carter and show their support. The crowd waited for Kennedy. And they waited. It took over fifteen minutes for Kennedy to appear. Reporters took the opportunity to discuss one more time the tension between the two candidates.

When Kennedy finally walked on, he raised his fist to the Massachusetts delegates. Then, he quickly shook Carter's hand and walked away after three minutes. Kennedy had practiced a more enthusiastic embrace but decided not to do it. Nor did he lift Carter's arm for the traditional sign of unity.[65] After Kennedy left, the crowd chanted "We Want Ted!" so vigorously that the senator returned to the stage for an encore. At that point, it looked like Carter had chased Kennedy down, only to have Kennedy merely put his hand on the president's shoulder.

Carter would never forgive Kennedy for failing to heal the divisions. Ronald Reagan, the Republican nominee, took close notice of what had happened. "If that's the best they can do in unity, they have a long way to go," he said.[66]

7

The Last Year

A recession is when your neighbor loses his job, and a
depression is when you lose your job, and recovery is
when Jimmy Carter loses his.

—Ronald Reagan (1980)

In the 1980 U.S. presidential election, President Carter was up
against not just a candidate but an entire movement. Ronald Reagan
was a product of modern conservatism. When Congress hunted
for communists in Hollywood between 1947 and 1952, Reagan, as
president of the Screen Actors Guild, cooperated with the investigation. In the 1950s, the actor, his political interests growing, soaked
up the writings of conservative intellectuals such as William F.
Buckley Jr., the founder of the *National Review,* and he was a regular reader of right-wing magazines like *Human Events.* But it was as
spokesperson for General Electric in the late 1950s, delivering
speeches across the country, that Reagan really honed many of his
ideas about the virtues of free-market capitalism, the dangers of
government intervention, and the urgency of anticommunism. His
transformation from New Dealer to modern conservative complete, Reagan officially switched parties in 1962. Two years later,

he delivered a dramatic televised speech for Senator Barry Gold-water during Goldwater's presidential campaign and caught the eye of younger conservative Republicans looking to take control of the party from their more moderate northeastern brethren. The speech, in which Reagan articulated the key conservative ideas of the American right, elicited more excitement than Goldwater, excitement that made Reagan the pick of California Republicans for governor from 1966 to 1974, one of the first conservative-movement politicians to win such a prestigious post.

On June 12, 1980, Carter advisers Tim Kraft and Les Francis convened a meeting with Democrats from California who had worked with Reagan when he served as governor of the state. Attendees discussed Reagan's main vulnerabilities: the fact that Reagan did not work hard, had developed few close personal friendships in government, and had a temper—although he had learned to control it in public. On the positive side, they stressed that his opponents always underestimated Reagan. "Shrewd," Jordan wrote in a memo about the candidate, "is the word used by these men who have known him for so long." They agreed that Reagan was a "very effective 'communicator' " who "has an uncanny ability to say things in a way that appeals to a broad spectrum of the voters. True, it is almost always simplistic and sometimes wrong, but people hear him, like him and believe him."[1]

Reagan's weakest point, immediately seized upon by the Carter campaign, was his proclivity to make embarrassing gaffes. Reagan, who would turn seventy in his first year in office, constantly raised the eyebrows of reporters. During the primaries, he answered "Who?" when Tom Brokaw asked him a question about Giscard d'Estaing, the president of France.[2] He once dismissed questions about his record on environmental legislation by stating that trees were the cause of air pollution. One of Carter's ads featured Californians telling the camera that they would hate to see Reagan in office, especially, as one person said, with his "ill-informed, shoot-from-the-hip types of comments."[3]

Carter's team felt Reagan's gaffes gave them a significant advantage. Caddell, looking through his most recent polls, sounded uncharacteristically optimistic when he proclaimed that "if Reagan keeps putting his foot in his mouth for another week or so, we can close down campaign headquarters, doubts about him are growing, his lead is shrinking, and more and more people are wondering whether he's up to the job. If this impression hardens, he'll be out of the race."[4]

The most ambitious electoral objective of the GOP was to pick off key voting groups who had supported Carter in 1976: blue-collar workers, Jews, Catholics, and evangelical Christians. Reagan was optimistic that as a result of Carter's fractious relations with key Democratic constituencies, significant voter blocs would be up for grabs. Following the strategy that he'd used in the 1980 primaries, Reagan took up the mantle of the antiestablishment candidate, promising to remain loyal to the people rather than the politicians. Turning the image of the party as the champions of big business and wealthy Americans on its head, Reagan declared the Republicans to be "the party of Main Street, the small town, the city neighborhood, the shopkeeper, the farmer, the cop on the beat, the blue-collar and white-collar worker."[5]

The strategy produced uneven results, though it was increasingly successful for the GOP as Carter and the Democratic Congress were unable to improve economic conditions. Though most unions continued to support Democrats, Reagan received the endorsement of the Teamsters, the Professional Air Traffic Controllers Organization, and the National Maritime Union. And while many Catholics had voted the traditional Democratic ticket in 1976, they were unhappy with the direction of Carter's administration and found Reagan's rhetoric on social and cultural issues to be appealing. Evangelicals had voted for Carter in large numbers in 1976, and they still told pollsters that the president was their favorite, but many were finding themselves at odds with him since he had paid little attention to matters such as abortion. Meanwhile, conservative political elements in the evangelical movement, such as the preacher Jerry Falwell and his newly formed

Moral Majority, were emerging as a powerful political force.[6] The conservative activists were registering voters (Falwell alone claimed almost 3 million) who had not voted before, and they were squarely behind Reagan.

Carter quickly realized he needed to shore up his liberal economic credentials. The cornerstone of Carter's economic policies, the anti-inflationary program of the Federal Reserve, had done little to generate enthusiasm among key factions of the liberal coalition, namely organized labor, a fact that had helped Senator Kennedy go as far as he did in the primaries.

Carter had tried to demonstrate his concerns about the economic hardship facing so many Americans by proposing in August a series of targeted tax incentives, liberalized unemployment benefits, and small domestic measures. Rejecting the broad, across-the-board tax cuts being championed by the right, including Congressman Jack Kemp of New York, Delaware senator William Roth, and Reagan, the president warned that "in the heat of an election year, is not the time to seek votes with ill-considered tax cuts that would simply steal back in inflation in the future the few dollars that the average American taxpayer might get. . . . America needs to build muscle, not fat, and I will not accept a pre-election bill to cut."[7]

While many liberal Democrats thought these measures were inadequate, Carter did receive some unexpected praise. Senator Kennedy said the initiative "indicates a genuine concern for rejuvenating our economy and providing jobs for our workers," while Governor Hugh Carey of New York, whom Carter appointed to serve on the new Economic Revitalization Board, said the president was "savvy and brilliant."[8]

· · ·

Carter's team was staffed with veterans from his earlier campaign: Jordan, Caddell, Powell, Rafshoon, and Tim Kraft. Old hands at the campaign game, they understood that Reagan was not a political lightweight, but they were also optimistic about their chances.

On Labor Day, despite Carter's low approval ratings, polls showed that the two candidates were still even. The president was up against the reeling economy, the hostage crisis, and the continued fallout from the Soviet invasion of Afghanistan, but Carter believed that they could paint Reagan as a right-wing extremist and as someone who was unqualified to sit in the White House. "Reagan is different," Carter told a group in Independence, Missouri, the home of President Harry Truman, "from me in almost every basic element of commitment and experience and promise to the American people, and the Republican Party now is sharply different from what the Democratic Party is. And I might add parenthetically that the Republican Party is sharply different under Reagan from what it was under Gerald Ford and Presidents all the way back to Eisenhower."[9]

The president refused to believe that Americans would vote for a candidate who was so closely aligned with the right. Democrats were also confident that they enjoyed certain built-in advantages, namely the fact that more Americans identified with Democrats than with Republicans[10] and the interest group, media, and think tank world of Washington still leaned toward the left.

One of the signature themes in Carter's fall speeches was to emphasize that voters were facing a choice between peace and war when they entered the voting booth. The goal of the Democratic campaign was to turn Reagan into another Barry Goldwater, making similar claims as Lyndon Johnson did in 1964, notably that their opponent could not be trusted to control the nuclear arsenal. "When it comes time to decide something," the narrator of one ad intoned, "no matter how many advisers and assistants, a president can never escape the responsibility of truly understanding the issue himself."[11] The architects of the Carter campaign understood that economic and international conditions did not favor the president. Their best hope at victory was to destroy confidence in Reagan as a person.

The president abandoned the Rose Garden strategy that he had used in the primaries against Kennedy, feeling that he needed to be more aggressive if he wanted to defeat Reagan. Only by going on the road would he generate interest from the local media. Carter was also assertive in using the power of his office to build electoral support. He felt that President Ford had failed to do this in 1976, and he learned from the mistakes of his former opponent. The president distributed federal grants and project money to key electoral areas. Chicago, in the critical state of Illinois, received extensive budgetary largesse. There was also an overhaul of a ship at the Philadelphia shipyards where Carter sought to shore up his shaky support with blue-collar workers.

Without question, Carter was now running as the president, not as the maverick. He surrounded himself with the glory of the White House rather than running away from it. Throughout these two months, he marshaled all of the resources that he enjoyed in his position and tried to make the case to voters that he had the experience and skill to be commander in chief again. The humble Carter of 1976 was gone. The band now played "Hail to the Chief" wherever he appeared.[12]

. . .

Several developments in September boosted Carter's confidence. The Billygate scandal had finally quieted down as investigators found no evidence of legal wrongdoing. There were some signs of economic recovery and, finally, there was word from Iranian contacts of a possible framework for an agreement for the release of the hostages.[13]

The last opportunity presented Carter with his most difficult policy challenge. He had to handle the negotiations over Iran during the most heated moments of the campaign. Republicans were not making it easy. During the Republican Convention, Reagan adviser William Casey had warned a reporter from the *Washington Star* of an "October Surprise." He coined the term to describe some kind of resolution to the hostage crisis that would be offered right as Americans were preparing to vote, just as Carter had done with his press conference before the Wisconsin primary against Kennedy. Casey's staff went so far as to develop a computer simulation program that predicted how the revelation of an agreement would influence the election if it occurred on different days in October: they found that a resolution before October would have no effect, while a resolution between October 18 and 25 would give Carter a boost of 10 percent. Casey formed the October Surprise Working Group to collect rumors and information.[14]

In his memoirs, Carter recalled that it was impossible to disentangle Iran from election politics: "The most gripping and politically important [issue] was still the holding of American hostages in Iran. Earlier in the year, I had not considered the hostage crisis politically damaging to me. In many ways, it had helped rally the public to my side. Now, however, the grief I felt over the hostages' continued incarceration was mixed with the realization that the election might also be riding on their freedom."[15]

The negotiations with Iran started on September 9, when Secretary of State Edmund Muskie received a call from the West German ambassador. The ambassador informed Muskie that he had a contact from Iran who had been empowered to speak for the leadership of the country. Deputy Secretary of State Warren Christopher met with Walter Mondale and Zbigniew Brzezinski to review the list of issues that Muskie said had been discussed. Upon hearing the review of the information, Brzezinski feared this was a trap to embarrass the United States, as did Mondale, but Carter insisted they continue to talk.

Christopher met with the Iranian contact on September 15. Calling himself "the Traveler," Sadegh Tabatabai was not what Christopher had expected. He looked like a polished Western businessman. They met again two days later, and it seemed that the Traveler had received a positive response from his contacts back in Iran. Following the meetings, Christopher flew back to Washington and reported to Hamilton Jordan that "we have something. The man I met with was realistic and obviously ready to resolve this thing." After hearing the report on the exchange, the president concluded that they "might be only days away from having the hostages home."[16]

On September 22, the international situation took an unexpected turn when Saddam Hussein invaded Iran. Hussein hoped that Iran's weakened international standing, which had resulted from the hostage situation, created an opportunity to expand Iraqi influence in the oil-rich region. At first, there was some hope within the United States that Iran would release the hostages and concentrate all energies on the war. Instead, the Iraq-Iran conflict fueled anti-American sentiment among Iranians, who blamed the United States for the invasion. Negotiations also became more difficult because Iranian leaders were distracted.

As Carter navigated through the situation in Iran and Iraq, he was also struggling with a third-party candidate at home, John Anderson. Though a former Republican, Anderson's main appeal was to independent and moderate voters. He thus posed a significant challenge to Carter, but less so to Reagan, whose support lay in a growing, solidly conservative base.

Carter's main strategy was to ignore Anderson, refusing to talk about him with reporters and not doing anything to help him obtain media attention. While Reagan and Anderson agreed to participate in the first debate, hosted by the League of Women Voters on September 21, Carter refused to attend if Anderson was included. Reagan criticized Carter's decision not to participate, and the League of Women Voters considered placing an empty chair on the stage to embarrass Carter. Though the league decided in the end that this would be inappropriate, Carter's absence was noted by the candidates. Reagan did well in the debate, which was watched by somewhere between 40 and 60 million viewers. Without Carter present, Reagan was able to make Anderson appear to be farther to the left than he actually was, thus diminishing Anderson's appeal among educated and suburban independents, who were his natural constituency.

Meanwhile, Carter was not having much luck repairing relations with core Democratic constituencies. The president's problems with Jewish voters, for example, did not subside. In early October, administration officials produced a series of memos acknowledging that they had been unable to stabilize the traditionally Democratic Jewish vote, which was essential to New York and California and important in swing states such as Florida, Illinois, New Jersey, and Pennsylvania. According to one memo, "While many Jews are increasingly skeptical of Reagan . . . they have still not returned in historic numbers to the Democratic fold."[17]

Throughout September, there was little movement in the electorate. A large percentage of voters were undecided, and nothing seemed to be pushing them to either side. While Carter was unpopular, voters were still uncertain about whether Reagan was too inexperienced or too radical. A single big event or mistake could determine the outcome of the election.

If anything had the potential to shake things up, it was Iran. The negotiations restarted when the Iranians reconvened their meetings with Warren Christopher. On October 9, the Traveler sent an encouraging note to Christopher, who contacted the president to let him know that there were discussions of a concrete financial offer.

Republicans were continuing to warn of an October Surprise, a refrain that had become part of Reagan's campaign. By this time, William Casey was not only gathering information about potential deals, but also spreading disinformation and false data to reporters.[18]

One of Carter's advisers admitted that "the way the release is done and the way it is seen—particularly if people think it has been a manipulative exercise—are very important and could cause a real negative backlash."[19] Reagan spoke about the crisis for the first time in early October, telling reporters there was a chance that the hostages would be freed before the election since the Iranians favored Carter; his running mate, George H. W. Bush, made a similar claim, suggesting that Carter was desperate enough to do almost anything in order to gain support.[20]

Republicans took a more hostile tack with television ads like

"Safire," which began with a picture of one of William Safire's *New York Times* columns, entitled "The Ayatollah Votes." The narrator cites a "copyrighted story" in the paper that stated: "The smoothest of Iran's diplomatic criminals was shown on American television this weekend, warning American voters that they had better not elect Ronald Reagan. Ayatollah Khomeini and his men prefer a weak and manageable U.S. president, and have decided to do everything in their power to determine our election result." The images were of armed Iranians and the Ayatollah Khomeini.[21]

Carter's aggressive attacks on Reagan, which intensified toward the end of the campaign, triggered a backlash from the media. Many observers started to complain that Carter was being too nasty, as discussions of his "meanness" came to dominate press coverage and undercut his image of being a good person. Even Carter's own advisers privately admitted that he had a problem. The president was prone to making exaggerated claims, and in the heat of the campaign he had gone so far as to imply that Reagan was an outright racist and willing to launch a nuclear war if elected to the White House.

The criticism became so pronounced that Carter went on Barbara Walters's television show to apologize for some of the statements that he had made. But his self-imposed moratorium did not last long; two days after the show, during a speech in Florida, Carter said that Reagan would be a "bad thing" for the nation. He made yet another statement about how Reagan would "lead us into war." Carter's advisers agreed that the president should not apologize for things that his opponent also did, but they were frustrated by their boss's penchant for hyperbole, which distracted the media away from Reagan's own outlandish statements.[22]

While Carter stumbled, conservative organizations became more vicious in their attacks on every issue. Conservative groups, Carter complained, "accused me of being 'soft on communism,' betraying America by 'giving away the Panama Canal,' subverting the teaching of children by organizing a new Department of Education, encouraging abortion and homosexuality."[23]

· · ·

The final major event in the campaign was the debate in Cleveland, Ohio, on October 28. This time, the League of Women Voters decided not to include Anderson, whose support had fallen below the minimum threshold. Reagan had resisted debating Carter until mid-October. By that time, Reagan sought to break the deadlock in the polls and was more confident because of a successful appearance at the Alfred E. Smith dinner in New York City on October 16, an annual event to honor the former governor of New York. Reagan had used the event to make some jokes aimed at deflecting concerns about his age. Using a southern accent, he recounted an imaginary conversation in which Carter asked him why he looked younger in every photograph of him riding a horse. "Well, Jimmy, I just keep riding older horses," Reagan responded.[24]

Unknown to the public, Reagan campaign manager and future CIA director William Casey had given to James Baker, who was a top campaign adviser, a stolen notebook filled with briefing materials meant to prepare Carter for the debate with Reagan. David Stockman, who was sitting in for Carter in the mock debates to prep Reagan, used the material to play Carter's role. Casey later denied that he had given Baker the material. A House investigation in 1984 did not produce a conclusive answer as to who had leaked the briefing book to Reagan's campaign staff. Carter believed the leaked notebook hurt him in the debate. The most recent work suggests that an aide to Senator Kennedy, bitter about the primaries, turned it over to Republicans.[25]

When Reagan and Carter appeared on the stage in Ohio, Jordan was immediately concerned. According to Jordan's recollections, "Everyone was very quiet. Jody seemed destined to set a smoking record that night. The image of Reagan and Carter appeared on the screen. I didn't like what I saw: Reagan looking relaxed, smiling, robust; the President, erect, lips tight, looking like a coiled spring, ready to pounce, an overtrained boxer, too ready for the bout."[26]

The debate did not go well for Carter, though he demonstrated an impressive command of policy detail. When asked about the health care problems facing the nation, Carter reeled off a large series of figures and facts in a professorial manner, effortlessly moving through data about the gaps in health care coverage. Carter also criticized Reagan for having opposed the creation of Medicare in 1965.

While Carter was speaking, however, the cameras caught Reagan chuckling as he heard the president's words. When it was Reagan's turn to speak, he said, "There you go again," simultaneously dismissing Carter's command of the information and his critique of Reagan as too extremist, all the while mocking the serious posture of the president. He then explained his position on Medicare and why Carter was wrong.

For his final statement, Reagan delivered a powerful blow by asking a question that devastated Carter, urging Americans to consider whether they were better off in 1980 than four years earlier. Carter realized that he was doing badly, and he also sensed how carefully thought out Reagan's statements were. He recalled that Reagan had "memorized lines, and he pushes a button and they come out."[27] Carter still felt that his expertise would matter more. "The issues are more important than performance," he told one reporter.[28]

A few days later, in the early hours of the Sunday morning before the election, Carter was called back from the campaign trail in Chicago with news of a possible breakthrough in Iran. Prime Minister Rajai and President Bani-Sadr had been given the green light to negotiate. Warren Christopher reported that the negotiators had possibly found the framework for a solution. Carter's campaign advisers were not excited about flying him back to D.C., given that winning in Chicago was his only chance of taking Illinois, a key state in the Electoral College. But they didn't have much choice. If he stayed, he could very well miss a chance to end the standoff.

The president vividly remembered that particular flight back to

Washington, as he watched the sun rise from his window and contemplated whether this crisis could really come to an end. "My prayer," he recalled, "was that the Iranian nightmare might soon be over and that my judgment and decisions might be wise ones. . . . If the hostages were released, I was convinced my reelection would be reassured; if the expectations of the American people were dashed again, there was little chance that I could win."[29]

As the president flew back on Air Force One, he called his wife to explain that the chances that this solution would work were still uncertain. Rosalynn's excitement about the news diminished when her husband said, "It could go either way." When she asked, "The release of the hostages or the election?" Carter responded, "Both." Rosalynn felt for the first time that her husband might lose.[30]

After he reviewed the details of the compromise, Carter realized that there were still serious problems to resolve. "No one said anything," Jordan recalled, "but every single person in that room knew at that moment that the hostages would not be free by Election Day."[31] The biggest sticking point was that the Iranians were insisting on immunity from legal action by Americans, one item on which the president refused to budge. Mondale was convinced that the administration could no longer win the election. "Damn, damn Khomeini!" Rosalynn said.[32]

Carter went on television Sunday night to inform the American public that it was unlikely that a deal would be reached before the election. His intention was to be honest with the public and to stifle Republican efforts to make every decision seem political.

But the fallout from the speech was not good, as the announcement confirmed perceptions that Carter was unable to resolve the crisis and was paralyzed in dealing with Iran. Carter soon knew the speech had killed him. The failure to obtain the release of the hostages was highlighted by the media coverage of the anniversary of the start of the crisis, which happened to fall on Election Day. This had opened up the "flood of related concerns among the people that we were impotent," with Iran as well as the energy crisis, the economy, and Afghanistan.[33]

The last week of the campaign went horribly for the administration. The poll numbers turned against Carter as undecided
voters broke decisively toward Reagan. According to one poll,
almost 40 percent of those polled said they would vote for Reagan
because he was not Carter, rather than because he was a conservative or a Republican.[34] Caddell "was getting some very disturbing
public-opinion poll results," Carter noted in his diary on November 3, "showing a massive slippage as people realized that the hostages were not coming home. . . . Almost all the undecideds moved
to Reagan."[35] Whereas Reagan's campaign had originally concen-
trated on attracting the support of traditionally Democratic blue-
collar voters in northern industrial states, southern voters were
strongly indicating their support for the GOP.

Caddell called Jordan at 2:00 a.m. on the morning of the 1980
presidential election. Jordan, initially disoriented, soon realized
that Caddell wanted to give him the final poll results. Caddell
told Jordan that "it's all over—it's gone!" When Jordan asked him
to explain what he meant, Caddell responded, "The sky has fallen
in. We are getting murdered. All the people that have been waiting and holding out for some reason to vote Democratic have left
us." He somberly predicted, "It's going to be a big Reagan victory,
Ham, in the range of eight to ten points." He said that it was the
"hostage thing" that did them in with "all these last-minute developments about the hostages and all the anniversary stuff just served
as a strong reminder that those people were still over there and
Jimmy Carter hasn't been able to do anything about it."[36]

Although the race had been close until the final week, Reagan
won a larger Electoral College total than any other president except
for Roosevelt in 1936 and Nixon in 1972. Reagan received 51
percent of the popular vote, with Anderson winning 7 percent and
Carter 41 percent. A whopping 489 electoral votes went to the
president-elect, as Carter received a meager 49. Carter did not
perform well with the traditional Democratic constituencies,
including blue-collar workers, Catholics, Jews, and southerners.[37]
On the night of the election, Carter admitted, "I spent a major

portion of my time trying to recruit back the Democratic constituency that should have been naturally supportive—Jews, Hispanics, blacks, the poor, labor, and so forth."[38] Carter won only in the District of Columbia, Georgia, Maryland, Hawaii, Rhode Island, and Minnesota. Even New Jersey and Massachusetts went Republican.

In addition, Republicans won control of the Senate. Several well-known Democrats were defeated, with the help of conservative organizations, including liberal icons Senators George McGovern, Frank Church, and John Culver. Republican freshmen who were closely connected to the right wing of the Republican Party, such as Dan Quayle of Indiana and Frank Murkowski of Alaska, pushed the congressional GOP rightward. In the House, Republicans and conservative Democrats made significant gains that increased the size of the conservative coalition.

The president called Reagan unexpectedly early in the evening to concede, at 9:01 p.m., while the president-elect was still in the shower. Carter then appeared before supporters at around 9:50 p.m. to make his formal announcement. Jody Powell had warned the president to wait until the voting ended in California, but the president wanted to "get it over with." Speaker O'Neill saw this as one final act of disrespect to Democrats running for Congress because the polls were still open on the West Coast, and some voters would not come out once they heard the presidential election was over. O'Neill called Frank Moore and barked, "You guys came in like a bunch of jerks, and I see you're going out the same way."[39]

When Carter met with Reagan on November 20 at the Oval Office to brief him, the president spent over an hour with the man who defeated him. Reagan didn't say a thing or ask any questions. The president, who was baffled, asked Reagan if he wanted a notepad, to which Reagan replied no.[40] The meeting did not leave Carter with a very good impression of the incoming president. Reagan seemed a stark contrast to Carter's own proactive and detail-centered approach to policy making.

. . .

During the lame-duck period of his presidency, Carter continued to pursue policy. One of his most important pieces of legislation was the Comprehensive Environmental Response, Compensation, and Liability Act, which created the Superfund, a trust fund to be used for toxic cleanups. Congressional support for the bill had increased in response to a toxic waste site found in the Love Canal section of Niagara, New York. Carter also signed the Alaska National Interest Lands Conservation Act, which protected almost 56 million acres of land and rivers in Alaska. This was considered one of the biggest environmental measures in American history. "In my lifetime, I knew I wouldn't be able to get it undone," one Republican lamented.[41]

In his farewell address, which he delivered on January 14, Carter returned to the themes with which he had launched his term in office. "Today," Carter said, "as people have become ever more doubtful of the ability of government to deal with our problems, we are increasingly drawn to single-issue groups and special interest organizations to ensure that whatever else happens our personal views and our own private interests are protected. This is a disturbing factor in American political life." Carter went on to highlight three major issues. The first was the need to diminish the risk of nuclear war, a danger that he said is "becoming greater" as "the arsenals of the superpowers grow in size and sophistication and as other governments acquire these weapons." The second was to "protect the quality of this world within which we live" through environmental regulation. "If we do not act, the world of the year 2000 will be much less able to sustain life than it is now." And the final theme was human rights: "I believe with all my heart that America must always stand for these basic human rights—at home and abroad. That is both our history and our destiny."

In the final days leading up to the inauguration on January 20, Carter and his team worked frantically to find a compromise with

Iran. After ten weeks of difficult negotiations and two sleepless nights toward the very end, Carter's representatives struck a deal at 6:30 a.m. on the morning of the inauguration. At about 6:47, Carter, looking tired and staring around the room with bloodshot eyes, called Reagan to inform him that $12 billion in frozen Iranian assets had been wired to a secure bank and the fifty-two American hostages, 444 days after they were taken captive, would soon board airplanes in Tehran.

The person who picked up the phone told Carter that the president-elect was still sleeping and that he did not want to be disturbed. Carter could not believe what he heard. Carter's wife came in a few minutes later, finding her haggard husband, and told him that he needed to shave and get ready for the ceremony.

Reagan didn't wake up until 8:00, at which time Michael Deaver followed instructions and knocked on his door to let him know that "you're going to be inaugurated as President in a few hours." Reagan joked, "Do I have to?"[42] Carter called Reagan a second time at 8:31 and updated the new president about the situation in Iran. Reagan apologized for not having answered earlier and promised that his staff would not say anything until the hostages were released. Carter reiterated that there should be no announcement until they were safe. Putting down the phone, Carter mockingly joked to his staff when they asked what Reagan had said by responding that the new president had asked, "What hostages?"[43]

At 8:39 a.m., Carter was prepared to celebrate but was still dressed in his informal clothes and unshaven. Yet there was one final act of humiliation from the Iranians. The fifty-two hostages were loaded onto an airplane. But then the planes just sat on the tarmac. The president realized that the Iranians were not going to allow his administration to receive credit. Rosalynn came in just a short time before the inauguration, finding her husband on the phones, waiting for a resolution. She insisted that he get dressed and prepare for the ceremony.

With the hostages stuck in the airplanes, the Carters and

Reagans were driven to the inauguration. There was little conversation between the two men. They came from very different worlds. "Fortunately it's a short ride," Nancy Reagan said.[44] Reagan spent much of the ride discussing former Warner Brothers movie mogul Jack Warner. Later Carter asked Gerald Rafshoon, "Who's Jack Warner?"[45]

At 12:35 p.m., minutes after Reagan was officially sworn in as president, the Iranians released the hostages. Reagan's presidency could not have begun with a more picture-perfect moment. Carter received a phone call at 12:38 while he was driving in a limo with Mondale to Andrews Air Force Base. Hanging up, he turned to Mondale, uttering the words he had hoped to say for months, though they came just a few hours too late: "They're out."[46]

Carter and several other members of his administration flew to Germany to meet the hostages. The encounter was an emotional affair. A sense of relief filled the air. At a private meeting that lasted for eighty minutes, Carter hugged each of the hostages as tears filled their eyes. When the meetings were over, Carter condemned, with great anger, the "despicable act of savagery" that the Iranians had committed. Upon returning to the States, Carter could not ignore or forget the political consequences he had suffered. He told his longtime adviser Jordan, "Ham, if we had had a little luck back in March or April and gotten 'em out then, we might be flying back to Washington instead of Plains."[47]

Iran might very well have made the difference, but the broader political picture told another story. Carter had run as a maverick in 1976 and he governed as one for much of his presidency, failing to secure the support of many key segments of the Democratic coalition. When faced with the twin challenges of a strong opponent, who was connected to a vibrant grassroots movement, and a series of difficult policy crises, Carter's political standing collapsed. As Reagan's advisers realized, by 1980 Carter was running with the thinnest possible base of support, a fact that Republicans exploited to move conservatism into the White House.

8

Pariah Diplomacy

Carter is someone who believes that when you have a
problem with someone, you go talk to them. . . .

—Aaron David Miller (2008)

After his defeat, Carter returned to Plains, Georgia, to spend
some time back home and to figure out what he should do in the
next stage of his career. Carter was extremely young for an ex-
president, only fifty-six years old. He tried to resume the most
normal life possible. Residents in Plains would see him around
town, though he was now driven in a limousine and protected by
Secret Service agents. On his first day back in Georgia, decked
out in jeans and informal work clothes, Carter asked his limousine
driver to take him to the town of Americus. Carter was building
an addition to his home for storing political memorabilia and he
wanted to buy some wood.[1]

On October 6, 1981, Muslim extremists assassinated Anwar
Sadat during a military parade. Sadat had been struggling since
his government had cracked down on Muslim fundamentalists.
Carter was devastated to learn of the death of his close friend. In
Carter's mind, it was a tragic loss for the region, where Sadat's

immense diplomatic skills would be greatly missed, and for the world, which mourned for one of the architects of the Camp David Accords. It was also a sign, Carter feared, that militant opponents of peace were growing stronger in the Middle East. "It was a great personal loss for me," Carter later said, "and a severe blow to the prospects for peace in the Middle East."[2]

During the trip to Egypt for the funeral, which Reagan declined to attend, Carter became closer to former president Gerald Ford, with whom he traveled, along with Richard Nixon. As a result of the trip, Carter and Ford formed a close working partnership. The two former presidents would continue to work on commissions and task forces in the next decade.

Carter took a trip to the Middle East, where he reported having positive exchanges with the Syrian leader Hafez al-Assad, as well as Palestinian intellectuals. He had fewer good words to say about his meetings with Israeli officials. Carter believed that Israel, under the leadership of Menachem Begin, was becoming more intransigent about the Palestinians and increasingly opposed to making peace with Arab nations. As a result, Carter's public state-ments against Israel were becoming tougher. He wrote an article with Gerald Ford for *Reader's Digest*, in February 1983, which his opponents labeled anti-Israeli. The continued construction of settle-ments along the West Bank, Carter and Ford wrote, "has caused both of us deep disappointment and a sense of grave concern that is shared by many other stalwart supporters of Israel." According to the article, Arab leaders had told the former presidents "privately" that they were prepared to accept peace with the Israelis and that if Israel was willing to live up to the Camp David Accords, there would be progress. In Carter and Ford's opinion, Israel was to blame for the lack of progress toward peace.

When confronted by critics about why he was being tougher with Israelis than with a dictator like Syrian president Assad, Carter responded that it was necessary to put greater pressure on a democratic society and that dealings with dictators had to be done in private.

By this time, Carter had concluded that the cause of Palestinian self-determination needed to be his central diplomatic goal. U.S. government officials were willing to talk only to "official" Arab leaders, and Palestinian leader Yasser Arafat had been isolated as a terrorist. Carter, by contrast, felt it was important to negotiate directly with Arafat as a representative of the Palestinian people. Carter interpreted the intensifying violence among Palestinian youth in the territories as an understandable response to Israeli policies, thus focusing the blame more on the Israelis than the Palestinians. Carter stated this starkly to the Council on Foreign Relations, claiming that there were no substantive differences between the United States and the major Arab states over the issues of Palestinian self-determination and a withdrawal from the West Bank and Gaza, so that "Israel is the problem toward peace."[3]

As he reentered the public arena, one of the most important relationships for Carter was with Atlanta businessman Ted Turner, the creator of the CNN cable television network. The station went on the air in 1980 with the goal of providing a twenty-four-hour news channel through the relatively new medium of cable television. Turner liked Carter very much, and his network devoted extensive attention to the activities of the former president. CNN offered Carter an international platform to promote his ideas and maintain media attention even after his departure from Washington.

Just as Carter relied on the media in 1976 because he was not the preferred candidate of the party establishment and needed another way to reach voters, CNN was important to Carter after 1980 as it gave him a platform at a time when relations with the Democratic Party remained chilly.

. . .

On October 1, 1986, the Carter Center and the Jimmy Carter Presidential Library and Museum opened. The center had been operational since 1982, run out of Emory University, where Carter taught as a professor. While all presidents since FDR have created a library to house their records and memorabilia, Carter decided that he wanted to do something bolder.

The central mission of the center, run in partnership with Emory, was inspired by what Carter had achieved with Sadat and Begin at Camp David. Its designers wanted to create a site that would serve as host to international leaders from all over the world and where opposing sides would be able to hammer out the major conflicts of the day. Focusing on human rights, the center also sent teams overseas to facilitate negotiations and monitor elections. Other projects included a bold financial assistance program, Global 2000, which has helped impoverished nations stop the spread of disease and improve their agricultural techniques and production.

The Carter Center quickly turned into an independent hub of diplomacy. Before it opened, Carter had already hosted several widely publicized diplomatic initiatives in Atlanta. He and a team of well-respected experts had sponsored a major forum on the Middle East as well as another on SALT II. As a result, the Carter Center rapidly emerged as a major presence. To finance the center, Carter had raised funds from wealthy individuals, major corporations, especially Coca-Cola, as well as the MacArthur and Ford Foundations.

· · ·

The establishment of the center illuminated the main paths Carter hoped his postpresidency would take, but it was the presidency of George H. W. Bush (1989–1993), according to the biography of Carter since 1980 by Douglas Brinkley, that proved to be the critical period for Carter's reemergence onto the international stage. Bush's secretary of state James Baker, a realist in foreign policy, provided an opening shortly after Bush took office. Carter had maintained his good relationship with Panama long after the transfer of the Panama Canal, and Baker approached Carter with the hope of having his assistance in dealing with elections that were scheduled to take place there shortly.

The situation in Panama had been deteriorating since 1985. The corrupt government under General Manuel Noriega, a former U.S. ally who had become increasingly assertive toward the United States, was heavily involved in the drug trade. While elections were scheduled for 1989, few observers believed that they would be legitimately conducted.

The elections were important to the Bush administration because Baker and Bush were hoping to pursue a different set of policies than Reagan for the region. Baker and Bush were optimistic that they could form more stable alliances with Latin American governments to promote democratic politics and free markets, but the Panamanian elections would bring, Baker realized, the first crisis. He and Bush knew that Noriega would lose the election if it was fair and legitimate. Most observers assumed the process would be rigged in favor of Noriega.[4] In response to Baker's request, Carter traveled to Panama with a team of observers from the center to monitor the election.

On Election Day, Carter literally roved the country, even walking into polling stations and insisting on personally observing as votes were counted over the objections of Noriega's military officials.[5] Carter was disgusted by what he saw, including officials switching tally sheets for fake voting tabulations. Independent polls were showing that the opposition leader, Guillermo Endara, had won by a three to one margin.

When Carter delivered a speech in Spanish denouncing the corruption that he and his advisers had witnessed, Noriega ended all communication. Indeed, after efforts to reach out to Noriega and with reports of violence erupting on the streets, Carter appeared before the media and denounced the election as corrupt. He told reporters that the government was "robbing the people of their legitimate rights" and said that he hoped there was a "worldwide outcry" about what had happened. The speech had a huge impact.

Carter was extremely popular among the Panamanian people, far more popular than Noriega himself, and certainly more than Noriega's puppet candidate, Carlos Duque. Noriega was livid over Carter's remarks, which were uttered on Noriega's home soil. One of Noriega's intelligence operatives, standing next to Carter's Latin American expert, Robert Pastor, as Carter spoke, whispered in Pastor's ear that the two Americans needed to leave right away.[6] That night Carter and the monitors returned to Washington, at the same time that Noriega announced that his country was in a state of emergency.

The speech generated international praise for Carter and gave him credibility around the world. He had shown what the Carter Center could accomplish, assisting a Republican administration to see how democratic reforms were working. Carter was willing to take a stand against a government, even if his statement played into the arguments of a Republican president who was clearly prepared to use military force. As Carter feared, and opposed, Bush subsequently sent troops into Panama to have Noriega arrested and extradited on drug charges.

The next year, President Bush asked the Carter Center to assist the administration in Nicaragua, where the leader Daniel Ortega had personally invited Carter to help establish the ground rules and mechanisms for the election. The elections were scheduled to be held under the socialist Sandinista government on February 25, 1990. Carter learned from some of his mistakes with Panama. This time, he arrived earlier in order to have time to develop stronger relations with government officials and build stronger levels of trust. Carter met extensively with Daniel Ortega and Humberto Ortega, the defense minister.[7]

Carter was very critical from early on about how the Sandinistas were trying to intimidate and smear supporters of the opposition candidate Violeta Barrios de Chamorro, saying, for instance, that the Sandinista newspaper was publishing "totally fraudulent" letters allegedly written by her supporters. Even so, American conservatives denounced Carter's presence in the country, which had been at the center of Reagan's anticommunist policies and the Iran-Contra scandal, charging that Carter's aim was to make certain the Sandinistas were victorious.

The Carter Center set up an elaborate team of observers to monitor the election. The center's Council of Freely Elected Heads of Government helped to negotiate with the Sandinistas and Contra leaders as to the process through which the election would be conducted. The election was almost canceled a day before voting when it was discovered that the ink being used to stain voters' hands, to prevent double voting, could be easily cleaned off with Clorox, but Carter found a resolution that allowed the election to proceed.[8] Election Day itself was relatively smooth. "It's very solemn, like a Mass," Carter said.

Although most observers predicted the Sandinistas would win by a landslide, the Nicaraguans surprised the world, voting Ortega and the Sandinistas out of office and electing Violeta Chamorro. The election was seen as a nonviolent victory against socialism, a welcome extension of the collapse of communism in Eastern Europe, much of which had not included any bloodshed.

Perhaps more important than his monitoring of the election was how Carter helped achieve a peaceful transition. Carter and Rosalynn met with Ortega late in the evening on election night to deliver the bad news. Ortega responded in disbelief, asking how all of the internal polls as well as international observers (including most members of the Bush administration) could have been so far off the mark. Carter interrupted Ortega to say, "I can tell you from my own experience that losing is not the end of the world."[9] At this crucial moment, Carter, using his own personal story, convinced Ortega to step down from power peacefully and encouraged him to allow a smooth transition to begin. As with Panama, Carter once again received international praise for the role that he played in monitoring the election and convincing Ortega to relinquish power without resorting to violence.

The positive relationship between President Bush, Secretary Baker, and Jimmy Carter in 1989 and 1990 had been unexpected, but through this alliance the former president and the Carter Center gained newfound international standing. Carter had also defined his postpresidential mission through these efforts. By monitoring elections and pressing for human rights, he and his wife, as Rosalynn said, were working hard to complete the "unfinished business" of his presidency.[10] By assisting a Republican administration, Carter had demonstrated his ability to work in bipartisan fashion and find issues that avoided the Left-Right divide.

· · ·

Despite continued criticism for favoring the Palestinians, Carter was also making progress in the Middle East. In the summer of 1990, Carter became involved in a new round of negotiations with the Israelis. But in August 1990, international attention shifted toward the Persian Gulf with the Iraqi invasion of Kuwait. When the invasion took place, Carter's negotiations with the Palestinians were set back because Arafat announced his support for Iraq. Most of the Arab world did not agree with Arafat as they condemned Saddam Hussein's act as a blatant violation of national sovereignty and joined the U.S.-led international coalition against him. Carter continued to talk with Arafat throughout the Persian Gulf crisis and the buildup toward war. The Palestinian leader pressured Carter into trying to convince U.S. leaders that there was a connection to the Israeli crisis. Bush accepted some of this argument on his own, causing Arafat to believe that Carter had significant influence within the administration.[11]

Carter, who in 1980 had announced a doctrine that refocused U.S. policy on the Persian Gulf in response to the Soviet invasion of Afghanistan, opposed the rush to war. While condemning the Iraqis, he called on the Bush administration to allow economic sanctions to have more time to work and to engage in diplomacy.[12]

Covered closely by the press with each and every statement, Carter became the most prominent U.S. figure in the international community warning against war. Carter insisted that the

Iraqis were not planning to invade Saudi Arabia, so there was no urgency for United Nations members to take military action.

Yet Carter could not seem to slow down the drive toward military intervention. Though Democrats in Congress were making similar arguments about the need to wait, Republicans were able to persuade enough Democrats to vote with the House and Senate minority to grant authority to the president to use troops. Bush and most of the top officials in the cabinet were fully convinced that using the military was the best and only feasible course of action.

On November 19, Carter was so desperate that he decided to do something dramatic. Unknown to the public, he sent a letter to the leaders of the other governments on the UN Security Council, urging them to pursue negotiations and to avoid endorsing the use of force if Iraq did not withdraw from Kuwait by the UN's previously announced deadline of January 15. Carter's letter bluntly stated that these governments should not follow the United States and should instead offer their "unequivocal support to an Arab League effort, without any restraints on their agenda."[13]

Secretary of Defense Dick Cheney was furious when he learned about what Carter had done. "Writing it was just plain wrong," Cheney later said. "To go behind our backs and ask world leaders to denounce our war policy was reprehensible, totally inappropriate for a former president."[14]

Iraq did not withdraw its troops from Kuwait, and the United States attacked. Once Operation Desert Storm began, Carter faded quickly from the public arena. Although the war was shorter than most expected and Bush resisted invading Baghdad, Carter lamented that the United States had decided to use force so quickly. He also became increasingly pessimistic about the future of Arab-Israeli relations. When the war ended, Arafat's stature had greatly diminished as a result of his statements in favor of Iraq. Israel exited from the war emboldened, as part of the alliance that defeated Iraq. Moreover, the country had proven itself to be loyal to the United States by agreeing to not fire back at Hussein when the Iraqis shot Scud missiles right into Tel Aviv and other areas.

Inside Washington, there was a sense that Carter was willing to engage foreign leaders without the authorization of the White House. Carter would once again be seen as an outsider, a valuable negotiator but a potential liability for his independent ways.

· · ·

When Bill Clinton ran for president in 1992, he did not have a good relationship with Carter. Clinton wanted to package himself as part of a younger cohort of centrist Democrats who were willing to support the use of military force and who questioned the benefits of government intervention at home. Despite his own role in pushing Democrats toward the center, Carter's low popularity ratings as president as well as his controversial reputation at the Carter Center for negotiating with left-wing international forces were too damaging for a hawkish Democrat.[15]

This had consequences. In 1993, Secretary of State Warren Christopher and other State Department officials kept Carter out of the loop regarding negotiations with Israel and Palestinians for fear that Carter's previous statements would poison discussions if he were to become involved. As a result, Carter had to learn most of his information from Arafat and Assad, as well as other well-placed Arab sources.[16]

Notwithstanding his exclusion, Carter was thrilled when in August 1993 the discussions culminated in the Oslo peace accords, with Israel finally accepting sovereignty for the Palestinians in the West Bank and Gaza. As the negotiations reached their final stages, Arafat had privately consulted with Carter to ensure that he was making the right decision.[17] The agreements were signed on September 13 at a White House ceremony, with Carter in attendance. For Carter, to watch Palestinian leaders meet with the Israelis and see Arafat and Rabin shake hands was the best possible victory that could follow the 1978 Camp David Accords and his long-standing efforts to raise the legitimacy of the Palestinian cause.[18]

Carter and Clinton finally had a good meeting after the Oslo Accords, and they were able to move beyond some of their tensions. The meeting allowed Clinton to turn to Carter in the summer of 1994 when a crisis unfolded with North Korea. Tensions with North Korea had worsened in the early 1990s, when the North Koreans began producing plutonium waste, which can be used to build a nuclear bomb. The nuclear program violated the Nuclear Non-Proliferation Treaty, which North Korea had ratified in 1985, as well as an agreement with South Korea in 1991 for a nuclear-free peninsula.

Clinton found himself in a difficult situation when North Korea accelerated its nuclear program and refused to allow inspectors from the International Atomic Energy Agency, as they had previously agreed to do, to examine their sites. Clinton was worried that the North Koreans would sell their weapons to other countries and that they might actually use the weapons themselves. In the middle of 1994, Clinton had been preparing to send troops into the region and possibly launch a preemptive strike against the North Korean nuclear facilities, just as Israel had done against Iraq in 1981.[19]

The North Koreans, under Kim Il Sung, invited Carter for a visit to help end the standoff, but the State Department refused to authorize the trip. Clinton wanted to make certain that the North Koreans understood that the United States insisted that North Korea halt the production of nuclear weapons, nothing less. Clinton lobbied to build support in the UN Security Council to impose strict economic sanctions on the North Koreans until they agreed to comply, but Russia, China, and Japan all hesitated to back this measure. Public opinion polls in the United States showed support for the use of military force against the North Koreans, and most prominent foreign policy makers and journalists advocated taking a tough stand.[20]

Carter disagreed with the strategy of threats and sanctions. He believed that sanctions only hurt the poorest sectors of North Korea and that Kim would become more defiant if threatened by the United States. When Carter learned that Clinton did not have any alternative plan if Kim continued to develop nuclear weapons, other than sanctions or war, he grew more desperate to find a better outcome.[21]

On June 1, Carter called Clinton to find out more on the crisis and to see about whether he could offer his assistance. The White House briefed Carter on what was taking place. Carter followed up the meeting by requesting Clinton's permission for Carter to accept an invitation from the North Koreans to meet with them. Vice President Al Gore responded to Carter with strict instructions from the president, telling him on June 7 that he could go under certain conditions. Clinton decided to allow Carter to make the trip with the objective of finding out the status of the North Korean nuclear program and determining what type of resolution might be viable. Carter was also told to make it clear to the North Koreans that he was visiting as a private citizen. National Security Adviser Anthony Lake briefed Carter on June 10, emphasizing that "Carter's role was to offer them a way out. It was not to offer them a new American policy that turned everything around" and to make sure they understood that he was there without "any clear instructions or official endorsement."[22]

The meeting with Kim Il Sung in North Korea went smoothly. The North Korean leader personally gave Carter assurances that he was willing to adhere to the U.S. terms, though he also showed his willingness to openly lie on a number of occasions (such as when he denied knowing about the status of international inspectors still in North Korea). After their discussions, Kim agreed to abide by the U.S. terms to temporarily freeze nuclear weapons production and allow international inspections, as long as there were guarantees that the United States would not attack and an understanding that the U.S. government would stop pursuing sanctions.

Shortly after, as White House officials were meeting to discuss sending troops to North Korea, they were informed that Carter was appearing on CNN International to announce that an agreement had been reached. Carter also told the interviewer, Ralph Begleiter, that he hoped the United States would stop pursuing sanctions. He said he had gone to Korea to "prevent an irreconcilable mistake and one that would permanently isolate North Korea and prevent any resolution of this very important issue in peaceful terms."

Clinton officials were furious.[23] Carter's announcement of an agreement could totally undermine their strategy of threatening North Korea with the possibility of UN sanctions. In one interview, Carter had undercut the careful work that Clinton and his staffers had done for over a year. According to one senior diplomat, "The North Koreans had reiterated that a sanctions resolution in the U.N. would be the breaking point. . . . Carter didn't know where it stood but he wanted to make sure he killed it. He knew some countries were wavering and I think he figured that if he went on CNN and said we have the makings of a deal . . . it would cause any nation that was wavering to stand back and say, wait a minute, let's not rush to sanctions."[24] Clinton, who had not authorized Carter to promise or to say anything, believed that Kim was using Carter to stall on sanctions without agreeing to do anything new.

Scrambling to determine what to do, the administration decided that it would offer to move forward with Carter's deal under certain conditions, including redefining the terms of the freeze. The National Security Council explained to Carter that Clinton wanted a written and comprehensive agreement under its more stringent definition of a freeze. Though Carter was angry and thought this would cause the North Koreans to back out, Kim Il Sung agreed to the new terms, which became the outline of a deal.[25]

As with previous interventions overseas, Carter received national and international praise for having prevented war and having demonstrated his diplomatic skills. But in doing so, he continued to stir up political opposition, demonstrating his willingness to ignore directives from elected officials. When Carter returned to the

United States, Clinton did not meet him personally. Instead, Carter reviewed his trip with Anthony Lake, after having to wait in the White House reception area, where nobody had even officially greeted him, to have a short phone conversation with Clinton.[26]

Carter did not care. He made extremely optimistic statements to the press, telling reporters in the most direct way, "I personally believe that the crisis is over." Calling Kim "vigorous and intelligent," Carter told a reporter on CNN soon after the incident that the lesson of North Korea was that "we should never avoid direct talks . . . with the main person in a despised or misunderstood or condemned society who can actually resolve the issue."[27] While some experts condemned Clinton, and Carter, for negotiating with dictators who would never live up to their promises, public opinion was supportive.

In the end, Carter did help to establish the framework for an agreement. On October 21, the United States and North Korea signed a new pact on nuclear weapons based on Carter's work that year. North Korea agreed to freeze weapons production and gradually dismantle its nuclear facilities in exchange for assistance with the creation of facilities that could be used for peaceful nuclear power, an end to the economic embargo against them, and the development of normal diplomatic ties. The North Koreans agreed that international inspectors could do their work.

Throughout all of these efforts, both his successes and failures, Carter was building a powerful institutional base for his post-presidential career through the Carter Center. The Carter Center had become an influential site for international negotiations and allowed Carter to have a more active role than almost any president before him.

. . .

Foreign policy was not all that the former president spent his time doing. Since the early 1980s, he had participated in a program called Habitat for Humanity, where he joined volunteers to construct homes for citizens who could not afford them on their own.

Carter also worked on a major domestic program called the Atlanta Project. Run through the Carter Center, the objective of the project was to strengthen impoverished communities and foster working alliances between government and community organizations.

Carter was also a productive author, publishing a number of books, starting with his memoirs, which he wrote without the assistance of a ghost writer and published in 1982. One of his best sellers was called *Turning Point*. Released in 1992, the book recounted Carter's rise to power in Georgia politics and described how he joined a group of young southern Democrats to break the hold of the old guard Democratic establishment.

One of the highlights of this stage of his career took place when Carter received the 2002 Nobel Peace Prize. He had been nominated several times since 1978, the year that he had hoped to receive it for his work at Camp David, but did not, allegedly as a result of his missing the deadline for being submitted. At the time the honor was awarded, President George W. Bush's unilateral response to the terrorist attacks on the World Trade Center and Pentagon in 2001 was very much on everyone's mind. The Nobel Committee was not subtle about its position, announcing that "In a situation currently marked by threats of the use of power, Carter has stood by the principles that conflicts must as far as possible be resolved through mediation and international co-operation based on international law, respect for human rights, and economic development."

Over the years, Carter became more strongly committed to the Palestinian cause and seemed increasingly hostile to the government of Israel, which he blamed for refusing to stop settlements and adhere to the Oslo Accords. Four years after being awarded the Nobel Peace Prize, Jimmy Carter triggered a political firestorm with the publication of his book *Palestine: Peace Not Apartheid*. The book charged that Israel was creating an apartheid state similar to what had existed in South Africa as a result of conditions in the West Bank and Gaza.

"The United States," he wrote, "is squandering international prestige and goodwill and intensifying global anti-American terrorism by unofficially condoning or abetting the Israeli confiscation and colonization of Palestinian territories. It will be a tragedy—for the Israelis, the Palestinians, and the world—if peace is rejected and a system of oppression, apartheid, and sustained violence is permitted to prevail."[28] The book infuriated Jewish organizations, many of whom had not trusted Carter during his presidency and who had come to think even less of him since he left office.

Fourteen members of the advisory board at the Carter Center resigned. "You have clearly abandoned your historic role of broker in favor of becoming an advocate for one side," they said in their letter of resignation.[29] Alumni at Brandeis University, the secular Jewish institution that was founded the same year as Israel (1948), protested when some faculty members invited the former president to speak on campus.

At Brandeis, Carter told a packed auditorium of seventeen hundred people that "this is the first time that I've ever been called a liar and a bigot and an anti-Semite and a coward and a plagiarist." During the speech, Carter apologized for sentences that suggested that suicide bombings would cease when the Israeli government finally accepted true peace with the Palestinians, a statement that many said legitimated the use of violence against the Jewish state. Carter acknowledged the words were poorly chosen, yet he defended the central message of the book. Standing before a packed hall, Carter denied accusations that he was anti-Semitic, urging the audience to visit the territories themselves in order to evaluate the "plight of the Palestinians."

The controversy exemplified Carter's postpresidential career. Carter defiantly took unpopular stands about foreign affairs, but stands that he fervently believed in, displaying almost no concern about who would dislike him as a result. He had spent much of his time since 1980 traveling around the globe, attempting to nurture negotiations among warring factions. He was seemingly unafraid to issue tough statements against government leaders whom he did not like, even if they were American allies. Freed from the need to build political alliances, Carter seemed more comfortable in his postpresidential role than when he was in the White House.

Throughout these years, Carter was still wrestling with one of the defining dilemmas of his foreign policy since his time in the White House: how to combine the hard-nosed realism of détente, with its emphasis on negotiating with any leader or government at any time, and the idealism that defined human rights. Carter's human rights concerns led him to target and castigate governments. At the same time, he also talked with other reviled government officials, granting them a measure of legitimacy, in the name of averting war.

Carter emerged as a vocal opponent of President Bush, who he said was the "worst in history" in terms of foreign policy. Carter called the detention centers at Guantánamo a "terrible embarrassment and a blow to our reputation as a champion of human rights." In the middle of the war with Iraq, in April 2008, Carter tried to jump-start peace negotiations in the Middle East by meeting with the democratically elected Hamas parliament of the Palestinians and reporting that they were prepared for substantive negotiations with the United States and Israel. Carter saw Bush's policies as clearly hurting the Arab-Israeli peace process, saying, "This Administration has abandoned what has been in the past a bipartisan commitment to a relatively balanced position in trying to find peace. It's been an ostentatious alliance between the White House and the Sharon government, I think to the detriment of our nation's image and to the detriment of an eventual peace agreement."[30]

In an op-ed in the *New York Times*, entitled "Pariah Diplomacy," Carter explained his general outlook as it related to Bush by writing that "a counterproductive Washington policy in recent years has been to boycott and punish political factions or governments that refuse to accept United States mandates. . . . Through more official consultations with these outlawed leaders, it may yet be possible to revive and expedite the stalemated peace talks between Israel and its neighbors. In the Middle East, as in Nepal, the path to peace lies in negotiation, not in isolation."[31]

. . .

Carter's postpresidential career has been historic and polarizing. Carter's willingness to negotiate with the world's worst dictators and to single out the United States and its allies for criticism fueled conservative, and sometimes liberal, anger. Throughout his postpresidential career, Carter has promoted a style of aggressive pariah diplomacy rooted in the Camp David Accords of 1978. He firmly believes in the virtue of constant negotiation, in as many regions of the world as possible, to find nonmilitary resolutions to conflict. Over the decades, he has succeeded on a number of notable occasions when presidents were otherwise struggling. He also undertook election monitoring in fragile democracies and demonstrated how third-party organizations could be valuable in evaluating whether authoritarian governments were truly moving toward reform. Carter became an important voice for diplomacy and negotiation in an era when those concepts were marginalized in public debate. And as he had done while serving as president, Carter has refused to be constrained politically when pursuing his international agenda. Without the challenges that came with being in elected office, and with a substantial institutional base at his disposal, this ex-president has neared the end of his career as an enormously powerful figure on the international stage.

Epilogue

When Republican John McCain wanted to insult his opponent in the 2008 election, he warned that Barack Obama's presidency would be like a Jimmy Carter second term. The joke did not need any explanation. Democrats responded by pointing to the differences between Obama and Carter, not by defending the former president. Even as Carter became known for having one of the most active postpresidential careers in American history, his time in the White House remains a symbol of failed leadership. In contemporary political debates and in history textbooks, Carter is consistently remembered as a president who failed to articulate a compelling political vision and who was unable to hold his party together. The image of a worn-down Carter holed up in the White House desperately trying to resolve the Iran hostage crisis into the final hours of his term has become almost as iconic as the images of President John F. Kennedy and his brother Robert conferring about how to avert the threat of nuclear war during the Cuban Missile Crisis. With all the praise given to Ronald Reagan, there is a sense that Carter's implosion offered the opening that conservatives needed.

This memory of his presidency is not inaccurate. If FDR and Reagan demonstrated how to hold a fractious coalition together,

Carter's legacy was just the opposite. He left the Democratic Party in shambles and went down to decisive defeat in 1980.

Yet in evaluating Carter's record, it is essential to remember the politically tumultuous time in which he governed. Americans elected Carter to serve as president at a fraught moment for the Democratic Party. Democrats had come out of the turmoil of the 1960s deeply divided without any clear sense of direction. The struggles over Vietnam and civil rights had opened up irreparable rifts among the factions within the party, which had once remained united through its members' loyalty to New Deal policies and anticommunism. Congressional reforms that fragmented power after Watergate made it more difficult to contain these internal tensions.

Carter had to manage these divisions at a time when the nation also faced an enormous international economic crisis. The combination of inflation and unemployment devastated Americans, leaving them anxious about where they would find their next pay check and whether they would be able to afford basic needs. The shift of economic power toward Japan and West Germany, coupled with the oil crisis of the 1970s, left policy makers feeling that they had diminished power to control conditions at home. The hostage crisis in Iran and the Soviet invasion of Afghanistan generated similar anxieties about the ability of the United States to influence events abroad.

At the same time, a conservative movement reached the peak of its political momentum by the late 1970s. The movement had been gathering steam for several decades. But in terms of organization, money, and institutions, everything came together in this critical decade. The movement possessed think tanks, local activists, campaign committees, radio talk-show hosts, and more, all of which could be tapped into by Republican politicians when they wanted to give the incumbent Democrat trouble.

Within that difficult context, Carter was able to score some notable policy achievements that have been too often forgotten. Translating some of the enormous skills that he had demonstrated in the politics of campaigning—quickly adjusting to events, displaying a feel for the mood of the electorate, demonstrating a genuine willingness to take on the political establishment, and preventing his opponents from pinning him down within particular ideological stereotypes—Carter could impress Washington.

The president pushed for some of the most comprehensive energy programs that had ever been attempted and won support for a few of those policies, such as solar energy, that are today considered essential. The institutionalization of human rights offered a foreign policy agenda that generated excitement among those who were disillusioned by the cynical realpolitik of Richard Nixon and Gerald Ford. Most important, in the Middle East, Carter brokered a durable peace agreement between the Egyptians and Israelis that has lasted over three decades and that no other president has thus far been able to replicate. When push came to shove, Carter showed that he could play hardball in the rough waters of Washington.

Despite these accomplishments and despite the challenges he faced, however, Carter did not display the same skills in the politics of governance as he did in the politics of campaigning. His presidency exposed the huge gulf separating those two types of leadership skills. Through most of his presidency, Carter was unable to nurture strong relations with congressional Democrats or core Democratic constituencies, as too often he was unwilling to engage in the kind of deal making and compromises that were expected from the White House. Nor did he demonstrate a good feel for what steps were necessary to create programs that had strong political support. The very qualities that allowed him to campaign successfully as an antiestablishment politician, when translated into governance, made it difficult to build a durable political coalition to which he could turn in the crisis years of 1979 and 1980. His embrace of the complexity of policy allowed him to think beyond traditional political orthodoxies, but it also prevented him from conveying the kind of compelling ideological vision that voters sought in difficult times. In essence, Carter's interest lay in the challenges of presidential leadership rather than the challenges of being a party leader. He was willing to use his political position to push the nation through difficult choices, but he was less interested or successful in taking the steps that were needed to leave his party more united and in a stronger political position by the 1980 election.

By that time, Carter could no longer draw on the assets that had served him so well in earlier campaigns. Being the president during four difficult years quashed his ability to claim the status of an outsider. His shortcomings in the politics of governance had been exposed and became a campaign issue. His willingness to challenge his party's interests and ideas left too many Democrats lukewarm, at best, when he asked for their vote for reelection.

Once he was relieved from the responsibilities that came from governance and being a party leader, Carter was again able to play on his strengths as a person willing to make difficult and politically unpopular choices. He embarked on one of the most active postpresidential periods in American history. He did not stop getting in trouble for his controversial positions but, after 1981, his maverick tendencies were less of a hindrance as he no longer had to answer to voters, Congress, or the Democratic Party.

Notes

1: A MAVERICK POLITICIAN

1. Jimmy Carter, *Keeping Faith: Memoirs of a President* (Fayetteville: University of Arkansas Press, 1995), 19–20.
2. James M. Naughton, "Crowd Delighted as Carters Shun Limousine and Walk to New Home," *New York Times*, 21 January 1977.
3. "Sowing Seeds of Real Conflict," *Time*, 18 April 1977.
4. The origins of the story are told in Jody Powell, *The Other Side of The Story* (New York: Morrow, 1984), 103–8.
5. "Rabbit Photo Is Kept Secret," *New York Times*, 5 September 1979.
6. Bruce J. Schulman, *The Seventies: The Great Shift in American Culture, Society, and Politics* (New York: Free Press, 2001), 103.

2: NEW SOUTHERN POLITICS

1. Jimmy Carter, *An Hour Before Daylight: Memories of a Rural Boyhood* (New York: Simon and Schuster, 2001), 15.
2. Kenneth E. Morris, *Jimmy Carter: American Moralist* (Athens: University of Georgia Press, 1996), 70.
3. Peter G. Bourne, *Jimmy Carter: A Comprehensive Biography from Plains to Postpresidency* (New York: Scribner, 1997), 25; Carter, *An Hour Before Daylight*, 74.
4. Carter, *An Hour Before Daylight*, 59–60.
5. Bourne, *Jimmy Carter*, 34.
6. Rosalynn Carter, *First Lady from Plains* (Boston: Houghton Mifflin, 1984), 22.

7. Jimmy Carter, *Turning Point: A Candidate, a State, and a Nation Come of Age* (New York: Times Books, 1992), 55.

8. Bruce Mazlish and Edwin Diamond, *Jimmy Carter: A Character Portrait* (New York: Simon and Schuster, 1979), 115.

9. Carter, *First Lady from Plains*, 36.

10. Ibid., 49.

11. Betty Glad, *Jimmy Carter: In Search of the Great House* (New York: Norton, 1980), 87.

12. "Bigger Voice for Big Cities," *Newsweek*, 9 April 1962.

13. Carter, *Turning Point*, 41–42.

14. My account of this campaign draws on ibid., 84–95.

15. Ibid., 130.

16. Bourne, *Jimmy Carter*, 153.

17. Glad, *Jimmy Carter*, 103; Bourne, *Jimmy Carter*, 160.

18. Ibid.

19. Morris, *Jimmy Carter*, 179–80.

20. "Hamilton Jordan," *Guardian*, 30 May 2008.

21. Stuart Eizenstat, interview with Emily Soaps, 10 January 1981, Jimmy Carter Presidential Library (JCPL, Atlanta, Georgia), Exit Interviews, 1.

22. Adam Bernstein, "Trusted Press Aide Helped Carter Reach White House," *Washington Post*, 15 September 2009.

23. Morris, *Jimmy Carter*, 178.

24. James Wooten, *Dasher: The Roots and Rising of Jimmy Carter* (New York: Summit, 1978), 291.

25. Morris, *Jimmy Carter*, 185.

26. Glad, *Jimmy Carter*, 129, 131.

27. Editorial, "The New Era in Georgia," *New York Times*, 14 January 1971.

28. Wooten, *Dasher*, 307–14.

29. Bourne, *Jimmy Carter*, 206.

30. Glad, *Jimmy Carter*, 148.

31. Bourne, *Jimmy Carter*, 206.

32. Ibid., 188–203.

33. "New Day A'Coming in the South," *Time*, 31 May 1971.

34. Jeffrey K. Stine, "Environmental Policy during the Carter Presidency," in *The Carter Presidency: Policy Choices in the Post–New Deal Era*, ed. Gary M. Fink and Hugh Davis Graham (Lawrence: University of Kansas Press, 1998), 181.

35. Nelson W. Polsby, *Consequences of Party Reform* (New York: Oxford, 1983), 57.

36. Wooten, *Dasher*, 319.

37. Ibid., 320–21.

38. Jules Witcover, *Marathon: The Pursuit of the Presidency 1972–1976* (New York: Viking, 1977), 107–8.

39. Morris, *Jimmy Carter*, 195.
40. Editorial, "House in Order," *New York Times*, 23 January 1975.
41. Martin Schram, *Running for President, 1976: The Carter Campaign* (New York: Stein and Day, 1977), 63.

3: THE OUTSIDER WINS

1. Bourne, *Jimmy Carter*, 274–75.
2. Ibid., 273.
3. Ibid., 195–96.
4. Ibid., 196.
5. Witcover, *Marathon*, 201–2.
6. Ibid., 194–202.
7. Ibid., 278.
8. "Carter: Swimming Upstream," *Time*, 13 October 1975; "Taking Jimmy Seriously," *Time*, 1 December 1975.
9. Joseph Kraft, "Carter: The Media Candidate," *Washington Post*, 14 January 1976.
10. Jeff Greenfield, *The Real Campaign: How the Media Missed the Story of the 1980 Campaign* (New York: Summit, 1982), 19; Witcover, *Marathon*, 239.
11. Laura Kalman, *Right Star Rising: A New Politics, 1974–1980* (New York: Norton, 2010), 153.
12. Schram, *Running for President*, 26.
13. Bourne, *Jimmy Carter*, 289; Carter, *First Lady from Plains*, 123.
14. William Lee Miller, *Yankee from Georgia: The Emergence of Jimmy Carter* (New York: Times Books, 1978), 69–80.
15. Kalman, *Right Star Rising*, 156.
16. Steven Brill, "Jimmy Carter's Pathetic Lies," *Harper's*, March 1976, 77–88. See also Christopher Lydon, "Carter Now a Target of Critics," *New York Times*, 19 January 1976.
17. Witcover, *Marathon*, 233.
18. Glad, *Jimmy Carter*, 291.
19. Joseph Lelyveld, "News Media Magnify Campaign," *New York Times*, 23 February 1976.
20. Witcover, *Marathon*, 249; Schram, *Running for President*, 31.
21. William Chapman, "He Carried Most Social, Age, and Ideological Groups," *Washington Post*, 11 March 1976.
22. Bourne, *Jimmy Carter*, 302.
23. Andrew Young, *The Spiritual Memoirs of Andrew Young* (Nashville: Thomas Nelson, 1994), 120–21.
24. Schram, *Running for President*, 91.
25. Ibid, 100–101.
26. Ibid., 125.

27. Ibid.
28. Bourne, *Jimmy Carter*, 316.
29. Schram, *Running for President*, 146.
30. Powell, *Other Side of the Story*, 183–84.
31. Jules Witcover, "Carter Is Slowed but Delegates Grow," *Washington Post*, 27 May 1976.
32. Witcover, *Marathon*, 349–50.
33. Schram, *Running for President*, 1–5.
34. William F. Buckley Jr., "The President Comes Alive with the Conservative Spirit," *Los Angeles Times*, 26 August 1976.
35. Schram, *Running for President*, 256–57.
36. Charles O. Jones, *The Trusteeship Presidency: Jimmy Carter and the United States Congress* (Baton Rouge: Louisiana State University Press, 1988), 33–34.
37. Steven M. Gillon, *The Democrats' Dilemma: Walter F. Mondale and the Liberal Legacy* (New York: Columbia University Press, 1992), 169.
38. Jones, *Trusteeship Presidency*, 35.
39. Schram, *Running for President*, 273.
40. Jones, *Trusteeship Presidency*, 35–36.
41. Schram, *Running for President*, 274–76.
42. Miller, *Yankee from Georgia*, 91.
43. Glad, *Jimmy Carter*, 321.
44. "Jimmy Carter: Not Just Peanuts," *Time*, 8 March 1976.
45. Patrick Anderson, *Electing Jimmy Carter: The Campaign of 1976* (Baton Rouge: Louisiana State University Press, 1994), 89–92; Kandy Stroud, *How Jimmy Won: The Victory Campaign from Plains to the White House* (New York: Morrow, 1977), 340.
46. Glad, *Jimmy Carter*, 379.
47. Schram, *Running for President*, 304–7.
48. Interview with Jimmy Carter, 28 April 1989, and interview with Gerald Ford, 11 November 1989, Debating Our Destiny Project, PBS Online.
49. Witcover, *Marathon*, 598, 604–5; Glad, *Jimmy Carter*, 391.
50. Robert David Johnson, *Congress and the Cold War* (New York: Cambridge University Press, 2005), 230–31.
51. Jones, *Trusteeship Presidency*, 45.
52. Schram, *Running for President*, 355.
53. Glad, *Jimmy Carter*, 401–2.

4: A YEAR OF PROMISE

1. Carter, *Keeping Faith*, 73–75.
2. Bert Lance with Bill Gilbert, *The Truth of the Matter* (New York: Summit, 1991), 84–85.

3. John A. Farrell, *Tip O'Neill and the Democratic Century* (Boston: Little, Brown, 2001), 449.
4. The MacNeil/Lehrer Report, Public Broadcasting Service, Online Archive, 21 January 1977.
5. Sean Wilentz, *The Age of Reagan, 1974–2008* (New York: Harper, 2008), 77.
6. Kalman, *Right Star Rising*, 181.
7. Glad, *Jimmy Carter*, 413.
8. "Warm Words from Jimmy Cardigan," *Time*, 14 February 1977.
9. Glad, *Jimmy Carter*, 409–13.
10. John Dumbrell, *The Carter Presidency: A Re-Evaluation* (Manchester, England: University of Manchester Press, 1993), 122.
11. Bourne, *Jimmy Carter*, 387.
12. Lance, *Truth of the Matter*, 73.
13. Morris, *Jimmy Carter*, 244.
14. Gillon, *Democrats' Dilemma*, 191–92.
15. Robert V. Remini, *The House: The History of the House of Representatives* (New York: Smithsonian Books, 2006), 453.
16. Dumbrell, *Carter Presidency*, 40.
17. Daniel Horowitz, *Jimmy Carter and the Energy Crisis of the 1970s: The 'Crisis of Confidence' Speech of July 15, 1979* (Boston: Bedford, 2005), 7.
18. E. C. Hargrove, *Jimmy Carter as President: Leadership and the Politics of the Public Good* (Baton Rouge: Louisiana State University Press, 1988), 49.
19. Leo P. Ribuffo, "'Malaise' Revisited: Jimmy Carter and the Crisis of Confidence," in *The Liberal Persuasion: Arthur Schlesinger, Jr., and the Challenge of the American Past*, ed. John Patrick Diggins (Princeton: Princeton University Press, 1997), 167.
20. Hamilton Jordan to President Carter, 1977, JCPL, Hamilton Jordan Papers, Box 34, File: Energy Legislation.
21. Carter, *Keeping Faith*, 146.
22. Scott Kaufman, *Plans Unraveled: The Foreign Policy of the Carter Administration* (DeKalb: Northern Illinois University Press, 2008), 64–65.
23. Carter, *Keeping Faith*, 284.
24. Hamilton Jordan, undated, JCPL, Office of Staff: Jordan, Box 35, File: Middle East (2); Jordan, June 1977, JCPL, Hamilton Jordan Papers, Box 34, File: Foreign Policy/Domestic Politics, HJ Memo, 6/77.
25. See material in JCPL, Domestic Policy Staff—Eizenstat, Box 235, File: Middle East Issues—Jewish Community (1).
26. Bourne, *Jimmy Carter*, 404.
27. Carter, *Keeping Faith*, 287.

28. Edward Sanders and Roger Lewis to Hamilton Jordan and Robert Lipshutz, 19 September 1977, JCPL, NSA, Brzezinski Country File—File: Israel 8–9/77.
29. Glad, *Jimmy Carter*, 422.
30. Thomas J. Sugrue, "Carter's Urban Policy Crisis," in Fink and Graham, *The Carter Presidency*, 142–49.
31. Joseph Kraft, "The First Hundred Days," *Washington Post*, 1 May 1977.
32. Gregory Paul Domin, *Jimmy Carter, Public Opinion, and the Search for Values, 1977–1981* (Macon, Georgia: Mercer University Press, 2003), 55.
33. Jones, *The Trusteeship Presidency*, 150–51.
34. Michael Schudson, *Watergate in American Memory: How We Remember, Forget, and Reconstruct the Past* (New York: Basic Books, 1993), 70–82.
35. Hugh Sidney, "Jimmy Behind Closed Doors," *Time*, 19 September 1977.
36. Carter, *Keeping Faith*, 132.
37. Walter LaFeber, *The Panama Canal: The Crisis in Historical Perspective*, updated edition (New York: Oxford University Press, 1989), 150–88.
38. George C. Herring, *From Colony to Superpower: U.S. Foreign Relations Since 1776* (New York: Oxford University Press, 2008), 837.
39. Jill Schuker to Joseph Aragon, 17 June 1977, JCPL, Office of the Chief of Staff, Box 36; Carter, *First Lady from Plains*, 165.
40. Hamilton Jordan, "Work Plan: Panama Canal," 28 June 1977, JCPL, Hamilton Jordan Papers, Box 34, File: Foreign Policy Issues Work Plans, 1977; Hamilton Jordan to President Carter, June 1977, JCPL, Hamilton Jordan Papers, Box 34, File: Foreign Policy/Domestic Politics Memo 6/77; Carter, *Keeping Faith*, 229.
41. John C. Barrow, "An Age of Limits: Jimmy Carter and the Quest for a National Energy Policy," in Fink and Graham, *Carter Presidency*, 167.
42. Mark Siegel to Hamilton Jordan, 3 October 1977, 5 July 1977, JCPL, Office of Staff: Jordan, Box 33, File: Patrick Caddell 1977 (1).
43. Powell, *The Other Side of the Story*, 58.
44. Glad, *Jimmy Carter*, 433; "Carter Wins the Approval of 54% and 30% in Gallup Poll Disapprove," *New York Times*, 17 November 1977.
45. David Harris, *The Crisis: The President, the Prophet, and the Shah—1979 and the Coming of Militant Islam* (Boston: Little, Brown, 2004), 75; David Farber, *Taken Hostage: The Iran Hostage Crisis and America's First Encounter with Radical Islam* (Princeton: Princeton University Press, 2005), 82.

5: CONSERVATIVES RISING, DEMOCRATS DIVIDING

1. Bourne, *Jimmy Carter*, 422.
2. David Skidmore, *Reversing Course: Carter's Foreign Policy, Domestic Politics, and the Failure of Reform* (Nashville: Vanderbilt University Press, 1996), 113.
3. Ken Bode, "Carter and the Canal," *New Republic*, 14 January 1978, 8.
4. Carter, *Keeping Faith*, 175.
5. William J. Jorden, *Panama Odyssey* (Austin: University of Texas, 1984), 459–61.
6. Glad, *Jimmy Carter*, 409–23.
7. J. Michael Hogan, *The Panama Canal in American Politics: Domestic Advocacy and the Evolution of Policy* (Carbondale: Southern Illinois University Press, 1986), 95.
8. Burton I. Kaufman, *The Presidency of James Earl Carter Jr.* (Lawrence: University Press of Kansas, 1993), 90.
9. Richard A. Viguerie, *The New Right: We're Ready to Lead* (Falls Church, Va.: Viguerie Company, 1981), 70–71.
10. Patrick Tyler, *A World of Trouble: The White House and the Middle East—from the Cold War to the War on Terror* (New York: Farrar, Straus and Giroux, 2009), 197.
11. Dumbrell, *Carter Presidency*, 126.
12. Raymond L. Garthoff, *Détente and Confrontation: American-Soviet Relations from Nixon to Reagan* (Washington, D.C.: Brookings Institution Press, 1985), 60.
13. Zbigniew Brzezinski to President Carter, 9 June 1978, JCPL, Zbigniew Brzezinski Donated Material, Box 41, File: Weekly Reports, 61–71.
14. Melvyn Dubofsky, "Jimmy Carter and the End of the Politics of Productivity," in Fink and Graham, *The Carter Presidency*, 106–7.
15. Edward M. Kennedy, *True Compass: A Memoir* (New York: Twelve, 2009), 359–62.
16. Kaufman, *Presidency of James Earl Carter Jr.*, 102–5.
17. Ann Dye to Frank Moore, 6 April 1978, JCPL, Office of the Congressional Liaison, Box 32, File: Memoranda 2/24/77–1/01/1980.
18. Ibid., 106–7.
19. Farber, *Taken Hostage*, 90.
20. Ibid., 5, 78.
21. William B. Quandt, *Camp David: Peacemaking and Politics* (Washington, D.C.: Brookings Institution Press, 1986), 204.
22. Powell, *Other Side of the Story*, 610.
23. Carter, *Keeping Faith*, 347.
24. Quandt, *Camp David*, 239.

25. Philip Hilsenrad to Hamilton Jordan, 21 May 1978, JCPL, Chief of Staff: Jordan, Box 48, File: Jewish Leaders.
26. Schulman, *The Seventies*, 133.
27. Dubofsky, "Jimmy Carter and the End of the Politics of Productivity," 104–5.
28. James Reston, "Carter at Midterm: Satisfied So Far But Ready to Admit His Mistakes," *New York Times*, 6 November 1978.
29. Bourne, *Jimmy Carter*, 424–25.
30. Editorial, "Any Hope for an Arms Treaty," *New Republic*, 25 November 1978, 5.
31. Kaufman, *Plans Unraveled*, 118.
32. John Barrow, "An Age of Limits: Jimmy Carter and the Quest for a National Energy Policy," in Fink and Graham, *The Carter Presidency*, 168; Hargrove, *Jimmy Carter as President*, 52–53.
33. Melvyn P. Leffler, *For the Soul of Mankind: The United States, the Soviet Union and the Cold War* (New York: Hill and Wang, 2007), 296.
34. Kaufman, *Plans Unraveled*, 183.
35. Farber, *Taken Hostage*, 98–100.
36. Leffler, *For the Soul of Mankind*, 301.

6: FALLING APART

1. "The State of Jimmy Carter," *Time*, 5 February 1979.
2. Schulman, *The Seventies*, 133–34.
3. W. Carl Biven, *Jimmy Carter's Economy: Policy in an Age of Limits* (Chapel Hill: University of North Carolina Press, 2001), 8.
4. Martin Tolchin, "Carter Aide Finds Limit to Party Aims," *New York Times*, 5 January 1979.
5. Gil Troy, *Mr. and Mrs. President: From the Trumans to the Clintons* (Lawrence: University of Kansas, 1997), 259.
6. Dumbrell, *Carter Presidency*, 98.
7. "State of Jimmy Carter."
8. Schulman, *The Seventies*, 134.
9. Zbigniew Brzezinski, *Power and Principle: Memoirs of the National Security Advisor, 1977–1981* (New York: Farrar, Straus and Giroux, 1983), 279–81.
10. "No Spirit of Camp David," *Time*, 12 March 1979.
11. Kaufman, *The Presidency of James Earl Carter Jr.*, 122.
12. Tyler, *A World of Trouble*, 236.
13. Carter, *Keeping Faith*, 429–30.
14. Quandt, *Camp David*, 289–90.
15. Edward Sanders to President Carter, 7 May 1979, JCPL, Special Advisor to the President—Moses, Box 10.

16. John C. Barrow, "An Age of Limits: Jimmy Carter and the Quest for a National Energy Policy," in Fink and Graham, *Carter Presidency*, 170–71.

17. "280 Seized at Rally at Nuclear Plant," *New York Times*, 30 April 1979.

18. Sugrue, "Carter's Urban Policy Crisis," Hugh Davis Graham, "Civil Rights Policy in the Carter Presidency," and Susan M. Hartmann, "Feminism, Public Policy, and the Carter Administration," in Fink and Graham, *Carter Presidency*, 137–57, 202–43.

19. Kevin Mattson, *"What the Heck Are You Up To, Mr. President?": Jimmy Carter, America's "Malaise," and the Speech that Should Have Changed the Country* (New York: Bloomberg, 2009), 65, 78.

20. Strobe Talbott, *Endgame: The Inside Story of SALT II* (New York: Harper, 1979), 53–54.

21. Garthoff, *Détente and Confrontation*, 730.

22. Ibid., 739.

23. Gaddis Smith, *Morality, Reason & Power: American Diplomacy in the Carter Years* (New York: Hill and Wang, 1986), 213.

24. Mattson, *"What the Heck Are You Up To, Mr. President?"* 33–47.

25. Ibid., 89–95.

26. Carter, *First Lady from Plains*, 325.

27. Jack W. Germond and Jules Witcover, *Blue Smoke and Mirrors: How Reagan Won and Why Carter Lost the Election of 1980* (New York: Viking, 1981), 33.

28. Clark Clifford with Richard Holbrooke, *Counsel to the President: A Memoir* (New York: Random House, 1991), 634–35.

29. Mattson, *"What the Heck Are You Up To, Mr. President?"* 131.

30. Mark J. Rozell, *The Press and the Carter Presidency* (Boulder: Westview, 1989), 113–56.

31. Clifford, *Counsel to the President*, 638.

32. Hedley Donovan to Zbigniew Brzezinski and Lloyd Cutler, 27 September 1979, JCPL, NSA, Brzezinski Material, Box 16, File: Cuba Soviet Brigade (Meetings) 9/79.

33. Farber, *Taken Hostage*, 139.

34. Ibid., 140.

35. Hamilton Jordan, *Crisis: The Last Year of the Carter Presidency* (New York: Putnam, 1982), 36–37.

36. Kennedy, *True Compass*, 369–71.

37. Hamilton Jordan to President Carter, 8 November 1979, JCPL, Hamilton Jordan Papers, Box 34, File: Iran 11/79.

38. Harris, *Crisis*, 268.

39. Farber, *Taken Hostage*, 152.

40. Jones, *Trusteeship Presidency*, 189.

41. Robert J. Donovan and Ray Scherer, *Unsilent Revolution: Television News and American Public Life* (New York: Cambridge University Press; Woodrow Wilson International Center for Scholars, 1992), 144.
42. Harris, *Crisis*, 268; Elizabeth Drew, *Portrait of an Election: The 1980 Presidential Campaign* (New York: Simon and Schuster, 1981), 76–123.
43. Germond and Witcover, *Blue Smoke and Mirrors*, 91–92.
44. Drew, *Portrait of an Election*, 124.
45. Andrew E. Busch, *Reagan's Victory: The Presidential Election of 1980 and the Rise of the Right* (Lawrence: University of Kansas Press, 2005), 64.
46. Ibid., 68.
47. Jordan, *Crisis*, 99.
48. U.S. Congress, Senate, 96th Cong., 1st sess., *Congressional Record*, 22 January 1980.
49. "Moscow Terms U.S. Steps Culmination of Anti-Soviet Trend," 16 January 1980, JCPL, NSA Brzezinski Material—Country File, Box 62.
50. Jones, *Trusteeship Presidency*, 189.
51. "Transcript of Kennedy's Speech at Georgetown University Press on Campaign Issues," *New York Times*, 29 January 1980.
52. Drew, *Portrait of an Election*, 123.
53. Francis Clines, "Carter Phone Drive Becomes Iowa Issue," *New York Times*, 5 January 1980.
54. Drew, *Portrait of an Election*, 142.
55. David S. Broder, "Leader of the Opposition," *Washington Post*, 26 March 1980.
56. Jordan, *Crisis*, 248.
57. Powell, *Other Side of the Story*, 219.
58. Jordan, *Crisis*, 199.
59. Busch, *Reagan's Victory*, 77.
60. Cyrus Vance, *Hard Choices: Critical Years in America's Foreign Policy* (New York: Simon and Schuster, 1983), 409–10.
61. Kaufman, *The Presidency of James Earl Carter Jr.*, 182.
62. Patrick Caddell to Les Francis, 26 May 1980, JCPL, Office of Chief of Staff, Box 77, File: Campaign Strategy—Ca.
63. Carter, *First Lady from Plains*, 331.
64. Busch, *Reagan's Victory*, 96.
65. Adam Clymer, *Edward M. Kennedy: A Biography* (New York: Morrow, 1990), 318.
66. Kaufman, *Presidency of James Earl Carter Jr.*, 195.

7: THE LAST YEAR

1. Jordan, *Crisis*, 303–4.
2. Greenfield, *The Real Campaign*, 85–87.
3. Television advertisement, "Streetgov," 1980, LivingRoomCandidate .org.
4. Jordan, *Crisis*, 338–39.
5. Gil Troy, *Morning in America: How Ronald Reagan Invented the 1980s* (Princeton: Princeton University Press, 2005), 43.
6. Busch, *Reagan's Victory, 107.*
7. Anthony S. Campagna, *Economic Policy in the Carter Administration* (Westport, CT: Greenwood Press, 1995), 181–82.
8. Steven Rattner, "Bid to Widen Voter Support," *New York Times*, 29 August 1980.
9. Carter, *Keeping Faith*, 563.
10. James Patterson, *Restless Giant: The United States from Watergate to Bush v. Gore* (New York: Oxford University Press, 2005), 149.
11. Television advertisement, "Oval Int," 1980, LivingRoomCandidate .org.
12. Drew, *Portrait of an Election*, 293–97.
13. Wilentz, *Age of Reagan*, 123.
14. Harris, *Crisis*, 382.
15. Carter, *Keeping Faith*, 566.
16. Harris, *Crisis*, 390.
17. Stu Eizenstat and Al Moses to President Carter, 30 September 1980, JCPL, Special Advisor to the President—Moses, Box 18, File: Campaign Strategy 9/30-80.
18. Ibid., 399.
19. George J. Church, "Battling Down the Stretch," *Time*, 3 November 1980.
20. Harris, *The Crisis*, 399.
21. Television advertisement, "Safire," 1980, LivingRoomCandidate .org.
22. Powell, *Other Side of the Story*, 48–49.
23. Carter, *Keeping Faith*, 570–71.
24. Edward Walsh and Lou Cannon, "Reagan and Carter Finally Brought Together," *Washington Post*, 17 October 1980.
25. James A. Baker III, with Steve Fiffer, *"Work Hard, Study . . . and Keep Out of Politics!" Adventures and Lessons from an Unexpected Public Life* (New York: Putnam, 2006), 118–120; Craig Shirley, *Rendezvous with Destiny: Ronald Reagan and the Campaign that Changed America* (Wilmington, DE: Intercollegiate Studies Institute, 1989).
26. Jordan, *Crisis*, 355.

27. Carter, *Keeping Faith*, 574.
28. "Both Sides Claim Their Man Won the Debate," *Los Angeles Times*, 29 October 1980.
29. Harris, *Crisis*, 407.
30. Carter, *First Lady from Plains*, 338.
31. Harris, *Crisis*, 408.
32. Troy, *Mr. and Mrs. President*, 271.
33. Carter, *Keeping Faith*, 577.
34. Michael Schaller, *Reckoning with Reagan: America and Its President in the 1980s* (New York: Oxford University Press, 1992), 33.
35. Carter, *Keeping Faith*, 577.
36. Jordan, *Crisis*, 365–66.
37. Busch, *Reagan's Victory*, 128.
38. Carter, *Keeping Faith*, 578.
39. Douglas Brinkley, *The Unfinished Presidency: Jimmy Carter's Journey Beyond the White House* (New York: Viking, 1998), 1–2.
40. Bourne, *Jimmy Carter*, 472.
41. Stine, "Environmental Policy during the Carter Presidency," 194–95; Brinkley, *Unfinished Presidency*, 25.
42. Richard Reeves, *President Reagan: The Triumph of Imagination* (New York: Simon and Schuster, 2005), 1.
43. Jordan, *Crisis*, 399.
44. Troy, *Morning in America*, 57.
45. Reeves, *President Reagan*, 2.
46. Harris, *Crisis*, 424.
47. Farber, *Taken Hostage*, 183.

8: PARIAH DIPLOMACY

1. Brinkley, *Unfinished Presidency*, 45. Chapter 8 relies heavily on Brinkley's account of this stage of Carter's career, the best single work on the subject.
2. Ibid., 66.
3. Ibid., 116.
4. Ibid., 276–77.
5. Ibid., 283.
6. Ibid., 285.
7. Ibid., 297.
8. Ibid., 305.
9. Ibid., 306.
10. Wayne King, "Carter Redux," *New York Times*, 10 December 1989.
11. Brinkley, *Unfinished Presidency*, 335.
12. Jimmy Carter, "The Time to Negotiate," *Time*, 22 October 1980.
13. Brinkley, *Unfinished Presidency*, 339.

14. Ibid.
15. Ibid., 351–52.
16. Ibid., 373–74.
17. Ibid., 377.
18. Ibid., 380–81.
19. Derek Chollet and James Goldgeier, *America Between the Wars: From 11/9 to 9/11: The Misunderstood Years Between the Fall of the Berlin Wall and the Start of the War on Terror* (New York: PublicAffairs, 2008).
20. Dan Oberdorfer, *The Two Koreas: A Contemporary History* (New York: Basic Books, 2002), 323.
21. Brinkley, *Unfinished Presidency*, 398.
22. Leon Sigal, *Disarming Strangers: Nuclear Diplomacy with North Korea* (Princeton: Princeton University Press, 1999), 152.
23. Brinkley, *Unfinished Presidency*, 403.
24. Sigal, *Disarming Strangers*, 158.
25. Brinkley, *The Unfinished Presidency*, 405–7.
26. Marion Creekmore Jr., *A Moment of Crisis: Jimmy Carter, the Power of a Peacemaker, and North Korea's Nuclear Ambitions* (New York: PublicAffairs, 2006), 221–27.
27. Sigal, *Disarming Strangers*, 166.
28. Jimmy Carter, *Palestine: Peace Not Apartheid* (New York: Simon and Schuster, 2006), 216.
29. "14 Carter Center Board Members Resign," CBS News, 12 January 2007.
30. Massimo Calabresi, "10 Questions for Jimmy Carter," *Time*, 8 December 2003.
31. Jimmy Carter, "Pariah Diplomacy," *New York Times*, 28 April 2008.

Milestones

—————

1924   James Earl Carter Jr. is born in Plains, Georgia.

1946   Carter graduates from the U.S. Naval Academy.

Jimmy and Rosalynn are married on July 7.

1952   Carter is accepted into the navy's prestigious nuclear submarine program.

1953   The Carters move to Schenectady, New York, where Jimmy takes classes at Union College.

James Earl Carter Sr. dies of cancer.

Jimmy, Rosalynn, and the family return to Plains.

1954   Supreme Court *Brown v. Board of Education* on May 17.

1962   Supreme Court *Baker v. Carr* on March 26.

Carter wins contested election to the Georgia Senate.

1966   Jimmy Carter loses the Democratic primary for the gubernatorial election on September 15.

1970   Carter defeats Carl Sanders in the Georgia Democratic primary for governor on September 9.

Carter wins the gubernatorial election on November 3.

1971   Jimmy Carter inaugurated as governor of Georgia.

State legislature passes government reorganization legislation.

1972   Following visit to the Democratic Convention, Carter and his advisers discuss the possibility of a presidential run in 1976.

Richard Nixon defeats George McGovern in landslide victory; Democrats retain control of Congress.

1973   Senate holds widely publicized hearings about Watergate scandal and campaign activities of the Nixon administration.

Democrats name Carter as the campaign chairman for Democratic National Committee on March 5.

1974   Richard Nixon resigns on August 8.

Congress passes campaign finance reform.

"Watergate Babies" elected to House and Senate.

Carter announces his candidacy for the U.S. presidency on December 12.

1975   Publication of *Why Not the Best?*

1976   Carter wins the Iowa caucuses on January 19.

Carter wins the New Hampshire primary on February 24.

Carter wins the Pennsylvania primary on April 27.

Carter wins the Ohio primary, while losing California and New Jersey, on June 8.

Democratic delegates vote for Carter as their candidate; Carter selects Walter Mondale as his running mate.

During the second televised debate on October 6, Ford denies that the Soviet Union controls Eastern Europe.

Carter defeats Gerald Ford to become president of the United States.

1977   Carter inaugurated as U.S. president on January 20.

Carter pardons Americans who avoided the draft during Vietnam on January 21.

Egyptian president Anwar Sadat meets with Carter on April 4.

Carter signs Reorganization Act on April 6.

Carter delivers televised speech to explain energy proposal.

Carter delivers the commencement address at the University of Notre Dame on May 22 in which he warns of America's "inordinate fear of communism."

House passes Carter energy plan on August 5.

Omar Torrijos Herrera, the president of Panama, and Carter sign the Panama Canal treaties on September 7.

Budget director Bert Lance resigns on September 21.

The United States and Soviets reach agreement on SALT II on September 27.

Carter signs the National Energy Act on November 9.

The shah of Iran visits Washington on November 15.

Anwar Sadat makes a surprise visit to Israel on November 19.

1978 Senate ratifies the Panama Canal treaties on March 16 and April 18.

The Camp David summit with Begin and Sadat begins on September 5.

Sadat, Begin, and Carter sign the Camp David Accords on September 17.

Congress passes energy legislation on October 15.

Carter announces the normalization of relations with China on December 15.

1979 The shah leaves Iran on January 16.

The Ayatollah Khomeini returns to Iran after being in exile in Paris.

The Egypt-Israel Peace Treaty signed on March 26.

Carter and Soviet premier Brezhnev sign SALT II on June 18.

Carter meets with experts at Camp David to discuss the crisis in confidence from July 3–12.

Carter delivers the "Malaise Speech" on July 15.

Carter requests that members of his cabinet resign on July 17.

Reverend Jerry Falwell forms the Moral Majority.

Reports that there are Soviet troops in Cuba in August.

At a meeting with the newly empowered Nicaraguan Sandinista leaders at White House, Carter offers millions in aid on September 2.

The shah of Iran is authorized to enter the United States for medical treatment on October 20.

Iranian students take over the U.S. embassy in Tehran on November 4; sixty-six Americans are taken hostage.

The Soviet Union invades Afghanistan on December 27.

1980   Carter delivers address to the country about the Soviet invasion.

Carter defeats Kennedy in the Iowa caucuses on January 21.

Carter introduces the "Carter Doctrine" on January 23.

U.S. boycotts Moscow Summer Olympics.

Failed U.S. secret mission to rescue the hostages in Iran on April 24.

Ronald Reagan accepts Republican nomination to be the presidential candidate on July 17.

Democrats nominate Jimmy Carter on August 13.

Iraq invades Iran in September.

Carter and Reagan hold their only debate of the election on October 28.

Reagan defeats Carter on November 4; Republicans gain control of the Senate while Democrats retain control of the House.

1981   Carter and the Iranians agree to the final terms for a release of the hostages on January 20.

Ronald Reagan inaugurated as president.

Iran releases the U.S. hostages on January 20.

1982   The Carter Center is founded.

Carter publishes *Keeping Faith*.

1983   Lillian Gordy Carter dies.

1990   Carter monitors elections in Nicaragua on February 23–28.

Carter monitors Haitian election on December 16.

1994   Carter travels to North Korea to discuss disarmament plan June 12–18.

1996   Carter heads delegation that monitors Palestinian elections on January 18–21.

2002   Jimmy Carter awarded Nobel Peace Prize.

Selected Bibliography

Abernathy, M. Glenn, Dilys M. Hill, and Phil Williams, eds. 1984. *The Carter Years: The President and Policy Making*. New York: St. Martin's Press.

Anderson, Patrick. 1994. *Electing Jimmy Carter: The Campaign of 1976*. Baton Rouge: Louisiana State University Press.

Baker, James A., III, with Steve Fiffer. 2006. *Work Hard, Study . . . and Keep Out of Politics! Adventures and Lessons from an Unexpected Public Life*. New York: Penguin.

Berkowitz, Edward D. 2006. *Something Happened: The Political and Cultural Overview of the Seventies*. New York: Columbia University Press.

Biven, W. Carl. 2002. *Jimmy Carter's Economy: Policy in an Age of Limits*. Chapel Hill: University of North Carolina Press.

Bourne, Peter G. 1997. *Jimmy Carter: A Comprehensive Biography from Plains to Postpresidency*. New York: Scribner.

Brinkley, Douglas. 1998. *The Unfinished Presidency: Jimmy Carter's Journey Beyond the White House*. New York: Viking.

Bronson, Rachel. 2006. *Thicker Than Oil: America's Uneasy Partnership with Saudi Arabia*. New York: Oxford University Press.

Brown, Harold. 1983. *Thinking about National Security: Defense and Foreign Policy in a Dangerous World*. Boulder: Westview Press.

Brzezinski, Zbigniew. 1983. *Power and Principle: Memoirs of the National Security Advisor, 1977–1981*. New York: Farrar, Straus and Giroux.

Busch, Andrew E. 2005. *Reagan's Victory: The Presidential Election of 1980 and the Rise of the Right*. Lawrence: University Press of Kansas.

Caldwell, Dan. 1991. *The Dynamics of Domestic Politics and Arms Control: The SALT II Treaty Ratification Debate*. Columbia: University of South Carolina Press.

Califano, Joseph A., Jr. 1981. *Governing America: An Insider's Report from the White House and the Cabinet*. New York: Simon and Schuster.

Campagna, Anthony S. 1995. *Economic Policy in the Carter Administration*. Westport, Conn.: Greenwood Press.

Carter, Jimmy. 1975. *Why Not the Best?* Nashville, Tenn.: Broadman.

———. 1992. *Turning Point: A Candidate, a State, and a Nation Come of Age*. New York: Times Books.

———. 1995. *Keeping Faith: Memoirs of a President*. Fayetteville: University of Arkansas Press.

———. 2001. *An Hour Before Daylight: Memories of a Rural Boyhood*. New York: Simon and Schuster.

———. 2006. *Palestine: Peace Not Apartheid*. New York: Simon and Schuster.

Carter, Rosalynn. 1984. *First Lady from Plains*. Boston: Houghton Mifflin.

Clifford, Clark, with Richard Holbrooke. 1991. *Counsel to the President: A Memoir*. New York: Random House.

Clymer, Adam. 1999. *Edward M. Kennedy: A Biography*. New York: Morrow.

Creekmore, Marion, Jr. 2006. *A Moment of Crisis: Jimmy Carter, the Power of a Peacemaker, and North Korea's Nuclear Ambitions*. New York: PublicAffairs.

Dayan, Moshe. 1981. *Breakthrough: A Personal Account of the Egypt-Israel Peace Negotiations*. New York: Alfred A. Knopf.

Derthick, Martha, and Paul J. Quirk. 1985. *The Politics of Deregulation*. Washington, D.C.: Brookings Institution Press.

Diggins, John, ed. 1997. *The Liberal Persuasion: Arthur Schlesinger, Jr., and the Challenge of the American Past*. Princeton: Princeton University Press.

Domin, Gregory Paul. 2003. *Jimmy Carter, Public Opinion, and the Search for Values, 1977–1981*. Macon, Ga.: Mercer University Press.

Donovan, Robert J., and Ray Scherer. 1992. *Unsilent Revolution: Television News and American Public Life, 1948–1991*. Cambridge: Cambridge University Press; Washington, D.C.: Woodrow Wilson Center for International Scholars.

Drew, Elizabeth. 1981. *Portrait of an Election: The 1980 Presidential Campaign*. New York: Simon and Schuster.

Dumbrell, John. 1993. *The Carter Presidency: A Re-Evaluation*. Manchester, England: University of Manchester Press.

Farber, David. 2005. *Taken Hostage: The Iran Hostage Crisis and Amer-*

ica's First Encounter with Radical Islam. Princeton: Princeton University Press.

Farrell, John A. 2001. *Tip O'Neill and the Democratic Century.* New York: Little, Brown.

Fink, Gary M., and Hugh Davis Graham, eds. 1998. *The Carter Presidency: Policy Choices in the Post–New Deal Era.* Lawrence: University of Kansas Press.

Foglesong, David S. 2007. *The American Mission and the "Evil Empire."* Cambridge: Cambridge University Press.

Frisch, Scott A., and Sean Q. Kelly. 2008. *Jimmy Carter and the Water Wars: Presidential Influence and the Politics of Pork.* Amherst, Mass.: Cambria Press.

Garthoff, Raymond L. 1985. *Détente and Confrontation: American-Soviet Relations from Nixon to Reagan.* Washington, D.C.: Brookings Institution Press.

Germond, Jack W., and Jules Witcover. 1981. *Blue Smoke and Mirrors: How Reagan Won and Why Carter Lost the Election of 1980.* New York: Viking.

Gillon, Steven M. 1992. *The Democrats' Dilemma: Walter F. Mondale and the Liberal Legacy.* New York: Columbia University Press.

Glad, Betty. 1980. *Jimmy Carter: In Search of the Great House.* New York: Norton.

Greenfield, Jeff. 1982. *The Real Campaign: How the Media Missed the Story of the 1980 Campaign.* New York: Summit Books.

Hargrove, E. C. 1988. *Jimmy Carter as President: Leadership and the Politics of the Public Good.* Baton Rouge: Louisiana State University Press.

Harris, David. 2004. *The Crisis: The President, the Prophet, and the Shah—1979 and the Coming of Militant Islam.* New York: Little, Brown.

Herring, George. 2008. *From Colony to Superpower: U.S. Foreign Relations Since 1776.* New York: Oxford University Press.

Hogan, J. Michael. 1986. *The Panama Canal in American Politics: Domestic Advocacy and the Evolution of Policy.* Carbondale: Southern Illinois University Press.

Horowitz, Daniel. 2005. *Jimmy Carter and the Energy Crisis of the 1970s: The "Crisis of Confidence" Speech of July 15, 1979.* Boston: Bedford.

Huyser, Robert E. 1986. *Mission to Tehran: The Fall of the Shah and the Rise of Khomeini—Recounted by the U.S. General Who Was Secretly Sent at the Last Minute to Prevent It.* New York: Harper and Row.

Jones, Charles O. 1988. *The Trusteeship Presidency: Jimmy Carter and the United States Congress.* Baton Rouge: Louisiana State University Press.

Jordan, Hamilton. 1982. *Crisis: The Last Year of the Carter Presidency.* New York: G.P. Putnam's Sons.

Jorden, William J. 1984. *Panama Odyssey.* Austin: University of Texas Press.

Kalman, Laura. 2010. *Right Star Rising: A New Politics, 1974–1980.* New York: Norton.

Kaufman, Scott. 2007. *Rosalynn Carter: Equal Partner in the White House.* Lawrence: University of Kansas Press.

———. 2008. *Plans Unraveled: The Foreign Policy of the Carter Administration.* DeKalb: Northern Illinois University Press.

Kreisberg, Paul. H., ed. 1985. *American Hostages in Iran: The Conduct of a Crisis.* New Haven: Yale University Press.

Kruse, Kevin. 2005. *White Flight: Atlanta and the Making of Modern Conservatism.* Princeton: Princeton University Press.

Kucharsky, David. 1975. *The Man from Plains.* New York: Harper and Row.

Lance, Bert. 1991. *The Truth of the Matter: My Life In and Out of Politics.* New York: Summit.

LeFeber, Walter. 1989. *The Panama Canal: The Crisis in Historical Perspective.* New York: Oxford University Press.

Leffler, Melvyn P. 2007. *For the Soul of Mankind: The United States, the Soviet Union, and the Cold War.* New York: Hill and Wang.

MacDougall, Malcolm D. 1977. *We Almost Made It.* New York: Crown.

Maddox, Robert L. 1984. *Preacher at the White House.* Nashville: Broadman.

Mattson, Kevin. 2009. *"What the Heck Are You Up To, Mr. President?": Jimmy Carter, America's "Malaise," and the Speech that Should Have Changed the Country.* New York: Bloomsbury.

Mazlish, Bruce, and Edwin Diamond. 1979. *Jimmy Carter: A Character Portrait.* New York: Simon and Schuster.

McCraw, Thomas K. 1984. *Prophets of Regulation: Charles Francis Adams, Louis Brandeis, James M. Landis, and Alfred E. Kahn.* Cambridge, Mass.: The Belknap Press of Harvard University Press.

McLellan, David S. 1985. *Cyrus Vance.* Totowa, N.J.: Rowman and Littlefield.

Miller Center of Public Affairs. Jimmy Carter Oral History Project.

Miller, William Lee. 1978. *Yankee from Georgia: The Emergence of Jimmy Carter.* New York: Times Books.

Moffett, George D., III. 1985. *The Limits of Victory: The Ratification of the Panama Canal Treaties.* Ithaca: Cornell University Press.

Morris, Kenneth E. 1996. *Jimmy Carter: American Moralist.* Athens: University of Georgia Press.

Muravchik, Joshua. 1986. *The Uncertain Crusade: Jimmy Carter and the Dilemmas of Human Rights Policy.* Lanham, Md.: Hamilton Press.

Oberdorfer, Don. 1997. *The Two Koreas: A Contemporary History.* New York: Basic Books.

Pastor, Robert A. 1987. *Condemned to Repetition: The United States and Nicaragua.* Princeton: Princeton University Press.

Patterson, James. 2005. *Restless Giant: The United States from Watergate to Bush v. Gore.* Oxford: Oxford University Press.

Polsby, Nelson. 1983. *Consequences of Party Reform.* New York: Oxford University Press.

Powell, Jody. 1984. *The Other Side of the Story.* New York: Morrow.

Quandt, William. 1986. *Camp David: Peacemaking and Policies.* Washington, D.C.: Brookings Institution Press.

Reeves, Richard. 2005. *President Reagan: The Triumph of Imagination.* New York: Simon and Schuster.

Remini, Robert V. 2006. *The House: The History of the House of Representatives.* New York: Smithsonian Books.

Rosenbaum, Herbert D., and Alexej Ugrinsky, eds. 1994. *The Presidency and Domestic Policies of Jimmy Carter.* Westport, Conn.: Greenwood.

Rozell, Mark J. 1989. *The Press and the Carter Presidency.* Boulder: Westview.

Sadat, Anwar. 1978. *In Search of Identity: An Autobiography.* New York: Harper and Row.

Safire, William. 1980. *Safire's Washington.* New York: Times Books.

Schram, Martin. 1977. *Running for President 1976: The Carter Campaign.* New York: Stein and Day.

Schulman, Bruce J. 2001. *The Seventies: The Great Shift in American Culture, Society, and Politics.* New York: Free Press.

Schulzinger, Robert D. 2002. *U.S. Diplomacy Since 1900.* 5th edition. New York: Oxford University Press.

Shirley, Craig. 2005. *Reagan's Revolution: The Untold Story of the Campaign That Started It All.* Nashville: Nelson.

Sick, Gary. 1985. *All Fall Down: America's Tragic Encounter with Iran.* New York: Penguin.

———1991. *October Surprise: America's Hostages in Iran and the Election of Ronald Reagan.* New York: Times Books.

Sigal, Leon V. 1998. *Disarming Strangers: Nuclear Diplomacy with North Korea.* Princeton: Princeton University Press.

Skidmore, David. 1996. *Reversing Course: Carter's Foreign Policy, Domestic Politics, and the Failure of Reform.* Nashville: Vanderbilt University Press.

Smith, Gaddis. 1986. *Morality, Reason & Power: American Diplomacy in the Carter Years.* New York: Hill and Wang.

Spear, Joanna. 1995. *Carter and Arms Sales: Implementing the Carter Administration's Arms Transfer Restraint Policy.* New York: St. Martin's Press.

Spencer, Donald S. 1988. *The Carter Implosion: Jimmy Carter and the Amateur Style of Diplomacy.* New York: Praeger.

Strong, Robert A. 2000. *Working in the World: Jimmy Carter and the Making of American Foreign Policy.* Baton Rouge: Louisiana State University Press.

Stroud, Kandy. 1977. *How Jimmy Won: The Victory Campaign from Plains to the White House.* New York: Morrow.

Talbott, Strobe. 1979. *Endgame: The Inside Story of SALT II.* New York: Harper & Row.

Thompson, Kenneth W. 1990. *The Carter Presidency: Fourteen Intimate Perspectives of Jimmy Carter.* Lanham, Md.: University Press of America.

Thornton, Richard C. 1991. *The Carter Years: Toward a New Global Order.* Washington, D.C.: Washington Institute Press.

Troester, Rod. 1996. *Jimmy Carter as Peacemaker: A Post-Presidential Biography.* Westport, Conn.: Praeger.

Troy, Gil. 1997. *Mr. and Mrs. President: From the Trumans to the Clintons.* Lawrence: University Press of Kansas.

———. 2005. *Morning in America: How Ronald Reagan Invented the 1980s.* Princeton: Princeton University Press.

Tyler, Patrick. 2009. *A World of Trouble: The White House and the Middle East—from the Cold War to the War on Terror.* New York: Farrar, Straus and Giroux.

Vance, Cyrus. 1983. *Hard Choices.* New York: Simon and Schuster.

Viguerie, Richard A. 1981. *The New Right: We're Ready to Lead.* Falls Church, Va.: Viguerie Company.

Wilentz, Sean. 2008. *The Age of Reagan: A History, 1974–2008.* New York: Harper.

Witcover, Jules. 1977. *Marathon: The Pursuit of the Presidency, 1972–1976.* New York: Viking.

Wooten, James. 1978. *Dasher: The Roots and the Rising of Jimmy Carter.* New York: Summit Books.

Young, Andrew. 1994. *A Way Out of No Way: The Spiritual Memoirs of Andrew Young.* Nashville: Thomas Nelson.

Zelizer, Julian E. 2004. *On Capitol Hill: The Struggle to Reform Congress and Its Consequences, 1945–2000.* New York: Cambridge University Press.

Acknowledgments

I would like to thank Dedi Felman for her outstanding work on this manuscript. Dedi was an exceptional editor who worked closely with me to highlight the key points of the narrative, to drop those parts of the story that were not essential to the narrative, and to bring alive some of the main characters and events of President Carter's career. It was a pleasure to work with her from start to finish. Thanks also to Sean Wilentz, the editor of the series, and to Paul Golob, the editorial director of Times Books, for inviting me to participate in this distinguished series and for their comments. As always, my literary agent Scott Moyers handled each stage of the process efficiently and with great care. In addition, I would like to thank Bruce Schulman and Meg Jacobs for their insightful comments on the book. Finally, Jake Blumgart was extremely helpful with his fact-checking work.

Index

Gordy, Bessie Lillian. *See* Carter,
    Bessie Lillian
Gore, Al, 140
Graham, Katharine, 40
Gray, James, 19
Griffin, Marvin, 15
Guantánamo detention centers, 145

Habitat for Humanity, 142–43
Halberstam, David, 56
Hamilton, William, 21, 28
Hammond, Doc, 16
Harkin, Tom, 62–63
Harris, Fred, 32, 36
Harris, Roy, 24
Hart, Peter, 67
Hartsfield, William, 14
Hefner, Hugh, 49
Herrera, Omar Torrijos. *See* Torrijos,
    Omar
Hertzberg, Hendrik, 97
Hollis, Annie Mae, 9
human rights
    Carter's foreign policy and, 2–3,
        61–62
    in the Soviet Union, 57–58, 62–63,
        70–71, 76–77
Humphrey, Gordon, 85
Humphrey, Hubert, 23, 29, 31
Hurst, Joe, 15–16
Hussein, Saddam, 118, 136
Huyser, Robert "Dutch," 87

inflation, 65, 83, 85, 88–90
Iran
    Carter's New Year's Eve in, 72
    Hussein's invasion of, 118
    Khomeini's control of, 90
    revolution in, 79–80, 87
    United States and, 72, 79
Iranian hostage crisis, 100, 101, 105–7
    Carter's presidential campaign and,
        102, 103, 105–6, 116–17, 128
    negotiations during, 117–18, 119,
        122–23, 126–27
    release of hostages, 127–28
Iraq, 118, 136–37, 145
Israel
    Carter's postpresidential
        negotiations with, 136
    Carter's public statements against,
        130, 131, 143–44
    conflicts with the PLO, 76
    Egypt and, 80–82, 90–92

Middle East peace agreement,
    63–65, 71
    Oslo Peace Accords and, 138
    UN resolution on settlements in
        occupied territories, 105

Jackson, Brooks, 3
Jackson, Henry "Scoop"
    Carter's support for, 27
    presidential primary campaign of,
        32, 33, 36, 39, 40, 41–42, 44
    on the Soviet Union, 62, 94
    support for an open Democratic
        Convention, 109
Jackson, Jesse, 96
Japan, 62
Jefferson-Jackson Day fund-raiser,
    34–35
Johnson, Haynes, 96, 101
Johnson, Lyndon, 5, 18, 54
Johnson, William Decker, 9
Jordan, Hamilton
    as assistant to the president, 55,
        64, 71
    as Carter's chief of staff, 98
    on Carter's health in 1978, 74
    on Congress, 58
    on debate between Reagan and
        Carter, 121
    as executive assistant to the
        governor's office, 24
    Iranian hostage crisis and, 88, 100,
        101, 106–7, 117, 123, 128
    on the "Israeli Lobby," 82
    on the personal element in politics,
        25
    role in Carter's gubernatorial
        campaign, 21
    role in Carter's presidential
        campaigns, 28, 37, 46, 50, 106,
        112, 114
    during Soviet invasion of
        Afghanistan, 103

Kahn, Alfred, 89
Kemp, Jack, 114
Kennedy, John F., 18, 19, 37, 147
Kennedy, Robert, 147
Kennedy, Ted, 29, 31, 43
    on Carter's budget cuts, 86
    Chappaquiddick scandal of,
        100–101
    at the Democratic Convention in
        1980, 110

Shriver, Sargent, 31–32, 36
Sick, Gary, 87
Siegel, Mark, 64, 70–71
Simon, Neil, 49
Singer, Sam, 16
Smith, Charlie, 14
Smith, Rosalynn. *See* Carter, Rosalynn
SNCC. *See* Student Nonviolent
  Coordinating Committee
  (SNCC)
Social Security Amendments (1977),
  71
South Africa, 63
South Korea, 139
Soviet Union
  arms agreements and, 63, 76
  brigade in Cuba, 98–99
  China and, 86, 95
  control of Eastern Europe, 51
  expansionism in Africa, 62
  human rights violations and, 57–58,
    62–63, 70–71, 76–77
  invasion of Afghanistan, 103, 136
  Khomeini and, 80
  view of Carter as a negotiating
    partner, 103–4
Soviet-U.S. communiqué, 70
special interest groups, 31,
  65–66, 93
Spock, Benjamin, 93
Stockman, David, 121
Stone, Richard, 98, 99
Strategic Arms Limitations Talks
  (SALT) treaties, 3, 57, 63, 76,
  94–95, 98, 99, 103, 132
Student Nonviolent Coordinating
  Committee (SNCC), 18
Superfund, 126

Tabatabai, Sadegh, 117
Teamsters, 113
Teeter, Robert, 45
Three Mile Island, nuclear meltdown
  at, 92

Thurmond, Strom, 56–57, 103
Time magazine, 26, 69, 88
Torrijos, Omar, 69, 70
toxic waste, 126
Troutman, Bobby, 19
Turner, Ted, 131
Turning Point (Carter), 143

Udall, Morris, 36, 39
UN Security Council, 105, 137,
  139
unemployment, 65, 66, 83, 89, 94
unions, 36, 77–78, 113
United Auto Workers, 36
urban reform, 66, 94

Vance, Cyrus, 56, 87, 100, 105,
  107
Vandiver, Ernest, 18
Veterans of Foreign Wars, 55
Vietnam War draft evaders, 55
Volcker, Paul, 104

Wallace, George, 22
  presidential primary campaign of,
    32, 39, 40, 44
  racist positions of, 32
  reaction to Mondale as Carter's
    running mate, 45
War Powers Act (1973), 55
Washington Post, 3, 40, 66, 105, 106,
  108
Wayne, John, 75
welfare reform, 4
West, John, 5
West Germany, 62
White Citizens' Council, 13
Why Not the Best? (Carter), 30
windfall profits tax, 92, 98
Winship, Thomas, 38
Woodcock, Leonard, 36
Wright, James, 54

Young, Andrew, 41

About the Author

JULIAN E. ZELIZER is the author or editor of nine other books, including, most recently, *Arsenal of Democracy: The Politics of National Security—From World War II to the War on Terrorism.* He is a professor of history and public affairs at Princeton University and is a regular contributor to CNN.com, nytimes .com, *Politico,* and other media. He lives in Princeton, New Jersey.